In Sanskrit, OM symbolizes Hinduism's divine principle.

The Greek abbreviation for Jesus often decorates churches.

Prayer call is given from a high Moslem minaret.

Grapes symbolize the blood of the Savior.

Hindu snakes even have own god.

The seven-branched menorah is familiar sign for Judaism.

Lotus is legendary wellspring of Hindu god Brahma.

THE WORLD'S GREAT RELIGIONS

LIFE SPECIAL EDITION FOR YOUNG READERS

TIME INCORPORATED

Editor-in-chief
HENRY R. LUCE

President
ROY E. LARSEN

"The World's Great Religions" Series and Book were produced
under the general direction of

EDWARD K. THOMPSON, *Managing Editor*
PHILIP H. WOOTTON, JR., *Assistant Managing Editor*
JOSEPH KASTNER, *Copy Editor*
MARIAN A. MACPHAIL, *Chief of Research*

by the following editorial staff:

Editor
SAM WELLES

Art Director
CHARLES TUDOR
BERNARD QUINT, *associate;* ALBERT KETCHUM, ROBERT YOUNG, *assistants*

Assistant Editor
OLIVER E. ALLEN

Writers
LINCOLN BARNETT, RALPH GRAVES, HENRY ANATOLE GRUNWALD,
EMMET JOHN HUGHES, PAUL HUTCHINSON, LIN YUTANG,
HENRY MOSCOW, WINTHROP SARGEANT,
DOROTHY SEIBERLING, CLAUDE STANUSH

Head Researcher
MONICA HORNE

Text of Special Edition for Young Readers
Especially Adapted by ARTISTS AND WRITERS PRESS, INC.
from the Original Version

Text and Picture Research by
JANE NELSON, JANE WILSON, VALERIE VONDERMUHLL; BARBARA ELLIS,
JOZEFA STUART, SUSAN NEUBERGER, MAYA PINES, WARREN R. YOUNG

Photographs and Illustrations by
DMITRI KESSEL, HOWARD SOCHUREK, GORDON PARKS, LYND WARD,
LEONARD MCCOMBE, ALFRED EISENSTAEDT, DAVID DOUGLAS DUNCAN,
CORNELL CAPA, FRANK LERNER, ANTONIO PETRUCCELLI,
BORIS ARTZYBASHEFF
(The names of other photographers and illustrators whose work appears
in this book will be found in the Picture Sources, page 189)

Editorial Assistants
ALBERT J. DUNN, ADRIENNE FOULKE, ROBERT E. FOY, EDWARD PUCCIA,
KAY CAMPBELL, LOIS RHOADES

Publisher
ANDREW HEISKELL

Assistant Publisher
ARTHUR R. MURPHY JR.

Book Manager
ROBERT L. BLACKMORE

Working closely with the above staff were also the following individuals
and departments of the magazine: Ray Mackland, Picture Editor; Irene
Saint, LIFE Newsbureau Chief; Helen Deuell, Copy Chief; LIFE's foreign and
domestic correspondents, picture bureau and copy desk.

THE
WORLD'S
GREAT RELIGIONS

by the Editorial Staff of LIFE

SIMON AND SCHUSTER

NEW YORK

CREDITS

LIFE is indebted to many authorities and institutions, notably those listed below, for their generous assistance in the preparation of "The World's Great Religions" Series and Book. However, LIFE assumes responsibility for the selection and arrangement of all the material in the book and the viewpoints expressed.

ALBRIGHT, DR. WILLIAM F.—W. W. Spence Professor of Semitic Languages, Johns Hopkins University

AUNG, U. HPE—New Buddhist Institute, Rangoon

BAINTON, DR. ROLAND H.—Titus Street Professor of Ecclesiastical History, Yale University Divinity School

BARR, ALFRED H., JR.—Director of Collections, Museum of Modern Art, New York

BISAR, DR. MOHAMED—Director, Islamic Center, Washington, D.C.

BRAUDE, RABBI WILLIAM G.—Temple Beth El, Providence, R.I.

BUSHY, DOUGLAS A.—National Council of The Protestant Episcopal Church, New York

CAMPBELL, JOSEPH—Professor of Literature, Sarah Lawrence College

CHAN, DR. WING-TSIT—Professor of Chinese Culture and Philosophy, Dartmouth College

CROSS, DR. FRANK M., JR.—Professor of Old Testament, McCormick Theological Seminary

DODGE, DR. BAYARD—President Emeritus of American University, Beirut

DWYER, S.J., REV. JOHN S.—Chairman of Department of Theology, Fordham University

EISENDRATH, RABBI MAURICE N.—President, Union of American Hebrew Congregations, New York

FATEMI, DR. N. SEIFPOUR—Professor of Social Science, Fairleigh Dickinson University

FLOROVSKY, THE RT. REV. GEORGES—Professor of Church History, Harvard Divinity School

FRIESS, DR. HORACE L.—Professor of Philosophy, Columbia University

GHINE, U OHN—Editor, *The Light of The Dhamma*, Rangoon

GINSBERG, DR. H. L.—Professor of Biblical History and Literature, Jewish Theological Seminary of America

GLUECK, DR. NELSON—President, Hebrew Union College-Jewish Institute of Religion

GOODRICH, DR. L. CARRINGTON—Dean Lung Professor of Chinese, Columbia University

GORDON, MRS. ANTOINETTE—Tibetan and Oriental Collections, American Museum of Natural History, New York

GRANT, DR. F. C.—Edward Robinson Professor of Biblical Theology, Union Theological Seminary

HALVERSON, DR. MARVIN P.—Executive Director, Department of Worship and the Arts, National Council of the Churches of Christ in the U.S.A., New York

HAMILTON, DR. CLARENCE H.—Professor Emeritus of Philosophy of Religion, Oberlin College

HAMILTON, DR. GEORGE HEARD—Professor of the History of Art, Yale University

HANDY, DR. ROBERT T.—Associate Professsor of Church History, Union Theological Seminary

HARDING, G. LANKESTER—former Director, Department of Antiquities, Government of Jordan, and former Curator, Palestine Archaeological Museum

HARRIS, DR. ERDMAN—Lecturer in Religion and the Fine Arts, Yale University Divinity School

HOENIG, DR. SIDNEY B.—Director of Adult Education and Professor of Jewish History, Yeshiva University

JACQUET, CONSTANT H. J.—Research Assistant, Bureau of Research and Survey, National Council of the Churches of Christ in the U.S.A., New York

JEFFERY, DR. ARTHUR—Executive Officer, Department of Near and Middle East Languages, Columbia University, and Union Theological Seminary

KAYSER, DR. STEPHEN S.—Curator of The Jewish Museum, New York

KAZANAS, REV. CONSTANTINE J.—Dean, Hellenic Cathedral of the Holy Trinity, New York

KNOX, DR. JOHN—Director of Studies, Union Theological Seminary

LIEBERMAN, DR. SAUL—Dean of Rabbinical School, Jewish Theological Seminary of America

LIU, DR. WU-CHI—Editor, Human Relations Area Files, Inc., Yale University

MAUNG, THE HON. JUSTICE U THEIN—Chief Justice, Union of Burma, Vice-President, Union of Burma Buddha Sasana Council

MUNSHI, DR. K. M.—Governor, Uttar Pradesh State, Republic of India

MURRAY, S.J., REV. JOHN COURTNEY—Editor, *Theological Studies*, Woodstock College

NIEBUHR, DR. H. RICHARD—Sterling Professor of Theology and Christian Ethics, Yale University Divinity School

NIEBUHR, DR. REINHOLD—Graduate Professor of Christian Ethics, Union Theological Seminary

NIKHILANANDA, SWAMI—Director, Ramakrishna-Vivekananda Center, Inc., New York

PARKER, DR. PIERSON—Professor of New Testament Literature and Interpretation, General Theological Seminary

QURESHI, DR. I. H.—Visiting Professor of History, Columbia University

RADHAKRISHNAN, DR. SARVEPALLI—Vice-President, Republic of India

RICHARDSON, DR. CYRIL C.—Washburn Professor of Church History, Union Theological Seminary

SAMARASEKARA, DHANAPALA—Social Affairs Officer, United Nations

SCHMEMANN, REV. ALEXANDER—Dean, St. Vladimir's Orthodox Theological Seminary

SICKMAN, LAURENCE—Director, The William Rockhill Nelson Gallery of Art and Atkins Museum of Fine Arts, Kansas City

SILVER, RABBI SAMUEL M.—Union of American Hebrew Congregations, New York

SKEHAN, MSGR. PATRICK W.—Professor of Semitics and Egyptian Languages and Literature, Catholic University of America

SOLOVEITCHIK, DR. JOSEPH—Professor of Talmud and Philosophy, Yeshiva University

TAO, FRANK—Editor, Chinese News Service

TILLICH, DR. PAUL J.—University Professor, Harvard Divinity School

TRAGER, DR. FRANK N.—Research Professor of Government, New York University

WALSH, MSGR. CHARLES M.—Director, Confraternity of Christian Doctrine, New York

WOLFSON, DR. HARRY A.—Nathan Littauer Professor of Hebrew Literature and Philosophy, Harvard University

YOUNG, DR. T. CUYLER—Garrett Professor of Persian Language and History, Princeton University

Acknowledgments to Institutions

AMERICAN BIBLE SOCIETY—New York

ARAB STATES DELEGATION TO THE UNITED NATIONS

COLUMBIA UNIVERSITY—New York

JEWISH THEOLOGICAL SEMINARY OF AMERICA—New York

METROPOLITAN MUSEUM OF ART—New York

NATIONAL COUNCIL OF THE CHURCHES OF CHRIST IN THE U.S.A.

NEW YORK PUBLIC LIBRARY

REPUBLIC OF INDIA INFORMATION SERVICES

ROMAN CATHOLIC ARCHDIOCESE OF NEW YORK

UNION THEOLOGICAL SEMINARY—New York

WILLIAM ROCKHILL NELSON GALLERY OF ART—Kansas City, Missouri

TABLE OF CONTENTS

HOW MANKIND WORSHIPS

by PAUL HUTCHINSON

Man is a religious being. His religion has taken endless forms. His names for gods and goddesses are numerous beyond counting. The rituals through which he has sought protection or blessing vary from the horrible to the sublime. But wherever and however he lived, from the time he became man, man has worshiped and has often shown a belief that he possesses an immortal soul.

This book does not present a history of man's religious evolution. Instead, this book explores the principal religions which are alive today, molding men's lives in all parts of the world as they try to impress their image on the history of our times. This book deals with religion as a living element in today's culture, not as a museum piece. What does man worship? And how? These are our questions.

COMMON ROOTS

To be sure, all religions of today have roots in the past. There is evidence of this on every side.

Jewish and Christian scholars find in the 4,000-year-old Babylonian epic of Gilgamesh striking parallels to the Biblical story of Noah. There is an ark covered with pitch, an enduring torrent of rain, the sending out of the raven and the dove, the ark landing on a mountain. This story helps us to see how much Hebrew culture, in growing up, took over from the older culture of the Tigris and Euphrates valley.

The Bible is a superb record of the growth of a religion. It begins with the story of a nomadic tribe, influenced by the civilizations of the Middle East and later of the Nile Valley. It shows the people of that tribe clinging, through weary wanderings, to their jealous tribal god, Jahweh. And it traces the growth of their religious belief as they roamed. It tells how they challenged and were sometimes attracted to the gods of the lands they touched. Then, as they settled in Palestine, their idea of Jahweh grew until He became the majestic yet forgiving and world-encompassing one God of the prophets and of Jesus.

It was this Jewish tradition, as we all know, which gave birth to Christianity. The young teacher, Jesus the Christ, built his stately teachings of brotherhood, salvation and love upon the firm foundation of his inherited Jewish faith.

And there is a third great religion which has grown from this same tradition of the nomadic Semitic peoples. It is Islam, often wrongly called Mohammedanism in honor of its prophet, Mohammed. He acknowledged his debt to Jewish-Christian sources, and listed Moses and Jesus among the prophets of his faith.

SIX GREAT RELIGIONS

While there are many religions in our present world, by far the most influential in the extent of their followings are the six with which this book mainly deals: Hinduism, Buddhism, the philosophies of the Chinese, Islam, Judaism and Christianity. The similarities between some of them are many; the differences are also many —in some instances they are fundamental.

But all six obviously have supplied answers to some of the great questions raised in every

◄ *God the Creator was pictured thus by the Italian Renaissance painter, Michelangelo, whose famous series of frescoes of Biblical subjects covers the ceiling of the Vatican's Sistine Chapel, in Rome.*

Balinese Hindus still burn corpses inside papier-mâché cows—clinging to this ancient animal-worshiping custom long centuries after accepting Hinduism—a religion in which cattle are sacred.

human mind by the mystery of life. All of them help men bear their sorrows. They all tell men how to live, and give assurance in the presence of death. The six have done these things with varying effectiveness. The present writer, a Christian, believes that Christianity has been the most effective of all. But all have brought answers to men's prayers. Otherwise, they would not be living religions. They all deserve our study and our respectful understanding.

THE NEED FOR TOLERANCE

There is a tendency in each of us to mock the unfamiliar in other men's faith and worship.

Such words as "heathen," "idolatry," and "superstition" are often used as insults. We hurl them at others; we seldom apply them to ourselves.

Yet every man should command respect in the moment when he bows before his god. We may believe that his view of the Divine lacks valuable, even essential, elements. His forms of worship may appear to us strange, sometimes offensive. But in that moment of prayer, every man is at his best. If we are as wise as we like to think ourselves, it is then that we will try to understand him. This book is an approach to such understanding.

Every great religion has noble teachings and lofty moral goals. Yet in each religion these high standards are often far removed from what that religion seems to be in the actual thought and practice of most of its followers. Do most Christians, for example, really live up to the teachings of Jesus?

Another aspect of this same problem is the wide gap which can open between the original teaching of a religion's founder (as nearly as it can later be determined) and what that faith has become after centuries of being worked over and interpreted by the founder's followers. Within each religion, there gradually grows up a wide spread of variations. By "Judaism," do we mean the traditional faith of Orthodox Jews, or the modernized beliefs of Reform congregations, or the middle-of-the-road teachings of Conservative rabbis? In Christianity, one cannot speak of the Roman, the Eastern Orthodox, the Anglican and the hundreds of Protestant churches as one and the same. Not all such distinctions can be drawn at every stage of this book. Yet the reader should always bear them in mind.

FAITHS IN THE FAR EAST

So this book on the great living religions tries to show all six of them as their believers now know them. It also quotes from their holy books, tells many of their sacred legends, and explains their traditional teachings in a way that makes clear the reasons for their present practices.

Thus we see that Hinduism, the mighty religion of India, is a faith which in Philip Ashby's words "is awakening from the sleep of the last centuries as it finds itself a central part of a new nation which is dreaming great dreams." Modern Hinduism is placing less emphasis on image-worship and its old taboos of caste, while exalting its lofty spiritual ideas. It is showing new concern, here and now, for the welfare of the unfortunate. And it is trying to provide a religious base for a young nation, India, anxious to take an important place in the world.

Hinduism, of course, has kept changing through the centuries as new leaders arose. In the sixth century B.C., Buddhism began as a revolt against orthodox Hinduism by Siddhartha Gautama, the Buddha. While Buddhism has now almost vanished from its native India, it may have as many as 500 million followers in the rest of Asia.

In Far Eastern religions, ideas concerning the nature of God have never been very important. Buddhism is devoted more to ethical living than to the gods. The Chinese philosophies are also mainly concerned with a man's way of life. Tao, the heart of Taoism, is "the way." Confucius, probably the greatest of the Chinese sages, did not teach of God as such. Instead, he taught a system of good conduct which has guided countless Chinese for over 2,500 years.

THREE RELIGIONS IN INDIA

There are, of course, other living religions. Because of the limited area of their influence, or the limited number of their believers, they are not treated at length in this book. Three of the most remarkable—the religions of the Jains, Sikhs, and Parsees—are in India.

Jainism, like Buddhism, was a revolt in the 6th Century B.C. against Hinduism. It started as a sect based on complete self-denial. Today its essence is *ahimsa,* or non-violence, the determination not to harm any living creature

of any sort. Jainism, with its million-and-a-half followers, is today showing new life. It is presenting itself as the way to universal brotherhood and the end of war.

The Sikhs—tall, turbaned, bewhiskered—are among India's most picturesque people. They have a militant faith which is one of India's youngest religions. It originated around 1500 A.D. and its founder, Nanak, was succeeded by nine generations of *gurus* (teachers) who compiled the Sikh scriptures. Most of the six million Sikhs live in the Punjab district.

The Parsees are a tiny group of not much over a hundred thousand. They are followers of Zoroaster, the Persian religious genius who lived about the 6th Century B.C. Zoroaster opposed the idea of any deity appearing in human form. He worshiped Ahura Mazda, the source of truth as symbolized by the pure light of the

Sikhs crowd a tent in New Delhi, India, to honor a religious leader—Har Krishen—their guru, *or teacher, from 1656 to 1664 A.D. Under the ornate central canopy a priest reads from the scriptures.*

Jain priests pour crimson powder over a 57-foot statue of the saintly Indian king, Gomateswara, who gave up the world for religion. Hundreds of thousands of devout pilgrims attend the ceremony.

sun. He warred against Ahriman, the dark spirit of evil. Parseeism entered India as a refugee faith, its followers fleeing before the Moslem conquerors of their Persian homeland. It has closed its ranks to outsiders, showing none of the missionary spirit now active in Hinduism, Buddhism, and Jainism. But the Parsees still have high ethics and believe in good works. Parsees follow the custom of disposing of their dead by leaving the corpses in "Towers of Silence" where their bones are swiftly picked clean by the hovering vultures.

OTHER RELIGIONS

Shinto, an ancient faith of Japan, claims at least part of the religious loyalty of many Japanese. It grew from early Japan's nature rites in which many things, including the famous mountain Fujiyama, were thought sacred. It devel-

oped into a family and patriotic faith, in which individuals worshiped their ancestors before tablets inscribed with ancestral names, and whole groups worshiped the state, usually in the person of the Emperor of Japan, who was considered divine. After Japan's defeat in World War II, the present emperor said he was not a god, and the future of Shinto in Japan's way of life is far from clear.

There are other living religions in the world, but most of them are the primitive beliefs of widely scattered tribes in North and South America, Africa, Australia and of the island dwellers of the Pacific and Indian oceans. Religion at this level has much to teach the anthropologist and the psychologist, but cannot be treated in such a book as this.

CHANGING TIMES AND FAITHS

No great new religion has swept into world prominence since Islam some 1,300 years ago. Does this mean that the above list includes all living religions? Yes, and no.

Through the centuries men have died for the right to believe. But other men, equally sincere, have died for the right to disbelieve. We must credit them with a kind of religious fervor. For atheism too is a faith in the sense that it is based on belief rather than scientific proof. In the Western world atheism, as meaning those who deny the existence of any and all gods, was more popular in the last century than it is now. It has yielded to the agnosticism which Robert Ingersoll summed up thus: "Is there a God? I do not know. Is man immortal? I do not know. One thing I do know and that is that neither hope nor fear, belief nor denial, can change the fact. It is as it is and it will be as it must be. We wait and hope." Believers such as the present writer may draw their own conclusions about the significance of that final sentence.

Since pure atheism and agnosticism obviously do nothing toward answering the ultimate riddles of life, some nonbelievers have turned to humanism—a term which has had varied meanings but which today, according to Corliss Lamont in *Humanism as a Philosophy*, "is the viewpoint that men have but one life to lead and should make the most of it in terms of creative work and happiness; that human happiness is its own justification and requires no sanction or support from supernatural sources; that in any case the supernatural, usually conceived of in the form of heavenly gods or immortal heavens, does not exist; and that human beings, using their own intelligence and cooperating liberally with one another, can build an enduring citadel of peace . . . upon this earth."

UNION OF FAITHS?

Often it is suggested that the major faiths should recognize their basic unity of purpose and drop their differences. They should, it is suggested, come together and merge in the beliefs on which they can agree. This call for a union of the faiths comes most often from the Orient, some of whose great religious reformers state that all religions are simply different paths to the same goal.

Certainly all the great religions can study and appreciate each other's spiritual values. But to erase all their differences, in overall unity, would mean for each a betrayal of their religious fundamentals. The man who calls for such

Shinto shrines customarily have brilliantly colored ornamental gateways, called torii. Here a row of them form a stately entranceway to the shrine of the goddess Inari at Fushimi, Kyoto, in Japan.

union always suggests—though he may not realize it himself—that everyone join around the essential core of his own faith.

COMMUNISM

And finally there has emerged in our times another great power over men's minds and acts—indeed, a faith—which is at once the denial of all religion and the most potent secular religion ever to challenge the other faiths. This is Communism, the political philosophy that dominates Soviet Russia, Red China and some other nations allied with them. Communism is a burning faith which is rapidly developing the structure and outline of a church.

Sikhs sit beside the Pool of Immortality before their Golden Temple at Amritsar. Their faith contains Islamic elements, but they hate Moslems, whose rulers martyred their great teacher, Arjun.

11

If, as a writer in the New Testament claims, faith is "the substance of things hoped for, the evidence of things not seen," then Communism —with its promise of a society where all are equal, and an equal sharing by all mankind in all the the benefits of life—surely is a faith. Like older faiths, Communism has its Revealers (Marx and Lenin), its infallible scriptures, its orthodoxy and its heresy, its saints and martyrs, its initiation rites and its consecrated burial grounds. It has its missionaries and its prelates. All it does not have today is its divinities. But give human nature another century or two—and the cynical gentlemen at the Communist controls as much time to manipulate it—and who can say that Marx, Lenin and Mao Tse-tung may not find themselves, to their amazement, among the gods? The same has happened to other agnostics.

In assessing Communism's brother pseudo-religions and cults such as nationalism, fascism and national socialism, Arnold Toynbee writes, "Religion is manifestly one of the essential faculties of human nature. No individual human being and no human community is ever without a religion of some kind; and, when people are starved of religion, the desperate spiritual straits to which they are reduced by being deprived of this necessity of life can fire them to extract grains of religious consolation out of the most unpromising ores."

The challenge of Communism will be felt through the whole world of religion. Perhaps the very abundance of its promises will prove its undoing unless within another generation it shows that its promises are within the reach of human performance. Until that day comes, however, the fervor of the Communist devotee will be a rebuke and a competition to every other religion which asks world acceptance.

PRESENT AND FUTURE

In their religious goals men do not differ much from one another, no matter where they live, or when. They seek the favor of their gods. They long for religious protection against the dangers of life. They desire spiritual community with their fellow human beings. They pray for courage in the hour of conflict, comfort in the hour of grief, guidance in their daily concerns. They want release from the pangs of conscience. And most—but not all of them—hope for some sort of immortality. The ways by which followers of the different religions pursue these common ends vary beyond all telling, though within all the great faiths there have been mystics who have risen above the level on which most of us live to a very similar sense of the Divine.

These are critical days for religion. The lives of people everywhere are rapidly changing, and even more enormous changes loom ahead. As man develops more power over the world around him, he must be saved from the most destructive of idolatries—self-worship. Each great religion in this book attempts to save man from following the road of self-worship to the City of Destruction. All will accomplish that purpose to the extent that, in the words of the prophet Micah, they inspire man "to do justly, and to love mercy, and to walk humbly with (his) God."

Thoughtful believers in a union of faiths—called syncretists—meet by the Ganges to hear a Hindu monk lecture on the oneness of all religions.

THE SPIRIT
OF HINDUISM

THE SPIRIT OF HINDUISM

Thousands of years ago, before Moses or Buddha or Christ had lived, sages stood on India's river banks and sang. Their songs, Hindus say, were inspired "by the breath of God."

Out of these chants—there were more than 15,000 stanzas in the earliest collection, known as the Rig Veda—and out of the wisdom and the spirituality of the sages since, has grown the religion known as Hinduism. It is the faith of more than 300 million human beings in India and of about 15 million more elsewhere. It has influenced thoughtful men of many lands through the centuries. Yet Hinduism has remained very much a puzzle to the West.

Its contradictions make it puzzling. It has one God, Brahman, who is the eternal spirit. But it also has 330 million gods—enough so that each family can have a favorite to honor at its household shrine. Some Hindus look upon all these as separate gods. But both modern philosophers and ancient Hindu sages say they are only the infinite aspects of the one Brahman.

Those ancient Hindu sages had pondered the fact that all things—even the granite of the mountains and the mountains themselves—disappear. They were struck, too, by the eternal recurrence of life: the life of the caterpillar ends, but it reappears as a butterfly. The butterfly dies, but its eggs hatch and soon there are more caterpillars. Any individual bit of life, the sages reasoned, must be born again and again. So must a human soul or self. It must pass from vegetable to animal, from animal to man, from one human body to another, up the scale, down the scale. And behind and within this changing material world must be the invisible source of life and of all things—pure and unchanging spirit.

So the sublime objective of Hinduism is to leave behind this harsh, material world and to be united with God. This union is reached not only through prayers and ritual but through the ideals of Hindu living: purity, self-control, detachment, truth, nonviolence, charity and the deepest of compassion toward all creatures.

At the end of this path waits Brahman, the universal God of whom the old scriptures—the Upanishads—say: "Thou art woman. Thou art man. Thou art the dark-blue bee and the green [parrot] with red eyes. Thou hast the lightning as a child. Thou art the seasons and the seas. Thou dost abide with all-pervadingness, Wherefrom all things are born."

The Universal Self
(A Hindu account of the creation)

In the beginning this universe was Self alone, in the shape of a person. He, looking round, saw nothing but his Self. He first said, "This is I"; therefore he became by name. Therefore to this day, if a man is asked, he first says, "This is I," and then says the other name which he may have. . . . In the beginning this was Self alone, one only. He desired, "Let there be a wife for me that I may have offspring, and let there be wealth so that I may offer sacrifices." Truly this is the whole desire, and, even if one wishes, one cannot get more than this.

—from the Upanishads

◀ Left: *A boy receives the sacred thread from his guru or teacher as a sign that he is now ready to accept the religious duties of an adult male.*

Aspects of the god Shiva. Shiva is the Destroyer who, in the endless turning of the world, clears away the old life to make room for the new. Here, in the Elephanta Caves near Bombay, sculptors of the 8th Century A.D. carved this 19-foot-high figure out of raw rock. In the center, according to one interpretation, is Shiva as the impersonal absolute. Emerging on the left is Shiva as male, and on the right as female. These represent the opposing forms in which life appears in the world.

TRUTH BEHIND A VEIL

Hindus use many forms and faces, symbols and myths to picture the many sides of God's oneness

The list of Hindu deities is like a museum of religion. For it includes almost every stage in the development of man's thinking about God.

The early gods, as in all primitive religions, personified the forces of nature: a sun god, a wind god, a god of fire. They still live on in Hinduism.

Then, as man began to be more aware of right and wrong, the god of the universe began to watch over men's behavior with his "eye" the sun. He rewarded the good and punished the bad, the sages taught. And gradually the idea grew up of one great god combining all the varied qualities of nature.

"Reality is one," declare the Vedas, the sacred songs of the Hindus. "Sages call it by different names."

Not only sages but most Hindu worshipers, even upper caste Hindus, still worship the one great central God by many names and in many forms. They have a multitude of nature gods, family gods, tribal gods.

The Hindu supernatural world is like a vast and wonderful fairyland. It swarms with gods resembling humans and animals, along with demons, heroes, ghosts and heavenly dancing girls.

A Daily Prayer

O Gods! All your names (and forms) are to be revered, saluted, and adored; all of you who have sprung from heaven, and earth, listen here to my invocation.

—from the Rig Veda

Many Hindus, especially among the lower castes, treat images of the gods as if they were human beings with all the needs and weaknesses common to humans. The worshipers give food to the images, bathe them, put dresses, jewelry and wreaths of flowers on them, and tuck them in bed at night.

DAILY WORSHIP

Every home has an altar and it is proper to offer some small gift, daily, to the gods. If you are too poor, as many Hindus are, to bring a bit of oil or milk, a flower or a scrap of ribbon, you may name in your mind the gifts you would like to offer and be given credit for the thought.

The thought is more important than the actual offering, as God is more important than the images. "One needs images and symbols," says one great Hindu teacher, "so long as God is not realized in His true form. It is God Himself who has provided these various forms of worship . . . to suit . . . different stages of spiritual growth and knowledge."

Religion is very much a part of the Hindu's daily life. There is a religious ritual for every act—for getting up in the morning, bathing,

Nearly every Hindu home has a shrine. This is the household altar of a devout Brahmin, who is seen here at one of his three periods of daily worship.

This large temple of Shiva rises at the edge of a village in South India.

cooking and eating meals. It is not proper, for example, to eat with a person of another caste. Even families do not usually eat together, for the wife serves her husband first, and eats later herself.

GROUPS WITHIN HINDUISM

There are dozens of sects within Hinduism, each loyal to a special god. There are countless *gurus*—religious teachers—to be seen all over India. They sit by the hour on the street corners of the cities, on the bypaths of the villages, surrounded by disciples and deeply interested onlookers, endlessly discussing fine points of their religion, as perhaps the sages did thousands of years ago.

Most Hindus, even though they may at the same time worship personal, family and village deities, become devotees or followers of either

Vishnu or Shiva. Theirs are the most important of the sects.

Vishnu the Preserver and Shiva the Destroyer, along with Brahma the Creator, keep the world turning. And the three of them are but three aspects of the supreme god, Brahman.

Those who devote themselves to Shiva are interested particularly in knowledge and self-discipline. They point out that their god's powers are not just destructive. It is necessary to be rid of the old to make room for the new. This Shiva makes possible.

Those who follow Vishnu think of him as a god of love. He has come to earth (or was made incarnate) as a human being a number of times, in order to overcome evil, according to Hindu teachings. The two general favorites among his incarnations are Rama, who is thought of as the ideal man, and Krishna, a

lovable hero. Many Hindus worship one or the other of these. The two are the heroes of many stories that Hindu children love.

THE POOL OF TIME

Hindus see time not as a flowing river but as a pool of water. Waves or ripples may appear, but the pool itself remains unchanged.

There is no purpose toward which the whole world appears to be working. There is no overall progress. There is only endless repetition. But within that repetition there are individuals making progress toward Brahman.

MAYA, THE WORLD WE KNOW

The world as we see it the Hindus call *maya*. It is just one fleeting bit of the vast universe of Brahman. Our world will last something over four billion, three hundred million human years.

Then it will be destroyed by fire or water and return to Brahman. But it will be recreated by Brahma the Creator—one of Brahman's many forms. For *maya* is a part of the endless cycle of life and must go on. It will be recreated thus endlessly, for the Hindus feel that nothing which really exists is ever absolutely destroyed. Things merely change form. Life in *maya*—in the visible world—takes infinite numbers of forms. It appears as men, animals, plants and minerals. It may be good or evil, male or female, pleasant or painful, hot or cold. But all those opposites, which are like veils between us and reality, are left behind when one reaches *moksha*. This is the state of peace and quiet within Brahman. When one has reached *moksha*, the world dissolves. People in this state have merged themselves into the oneness of things.

THE PRINCIPAL HINDU GODS AND DEMONS—*Most important of the gods are the trinity,
Brahma, Vishnu and Shiva (at the top). Beside Brahma the Creator (whose four heads indicate the breadth
of his mind) sits his peacock-riding wife, Sarasvati, goddess of the creative arts. Vishnu the Preserver (right)
is seen lying on Ananta, a multiheaded serpent, with his wife Lakshmi at his feet, and (below) he is seen in
some of the other forms in which he has appeared on earth. At far right are Vishnu's two most famous human
forms, Rama and Krishna. Radha, lover of young Krishna, is a mortal girl. Sita, Rama's wife, is a form of
Lakshmi. Rama's chief helper is the monkey god Hanuman.*

*Shiva the Destroyer (left) sometimes rides a bull holding his wife Parvati with one arm. He also dances
elegantly on a dwarf's back or sits meditating with the holy Ganges River spouting from the top of his head.
Shiva's wife, the mother goddess, has many forms too. As Parvati or Uma she is graceful and womanly. As*

*Durga she is fierce. And as Kali she is bloodthirsty. Shiva's sons are the warlike Karttikeya, leader of the gods'
armies, and the gentle, elephant-headed Ganesha, remover of obstacles, who has a rat for a helper.*

*On a lower level are (left to right) the twin Ashvins, physicians to the gods; Ushas, the dawn goddess, who
drives seven cows symbolizing the days of the week; Agni, god of fire, who rides a ram; Indra, thousand-eyed
god of the starry heavens; Chandra, the moon; Vayu, the wind god; and the Maruts, who are in charge of
stormclouds and are armed with thunderbolts.*

*Other supernatural beings on a still lower level are Ravana, the demon king; Manu, who, like Noah, sur-
vived a world flood; Soma, god of the sacred and intoxicating soma juice; Varuna, god of the cosmic order,
who rides Makara, a monster fish; the serpent Vritra, a chief enemy of the gods; Yama, king of death, who
is followed by two dogs as he drags souls into heaven and hell. The rest are minor gods, goddesses and demons.*

Non-Brahmin castes mingle in the villages and use the same well. Some work on Brahmin farms, but they do not enter Brahmin homes.

CASTE   *Society is divided by merits earned in past lives*

CASTE

Position in society is said to be fixed according to the merits one has earned in one's past lives. The pictures on these two pages, taken in the village of Kayar Colathure in southern India, show some of the many different positions.

At creation, certain humans came from the mouth of Brahma, and were granted the gift of understanding. They were the first Brahmins of the priestly caste. From his breast Brahma created others, who were full of strength and unconquerable. They became the Kshatriyas,

A caste fight starts when a defiant non-Brahmin waters his oxen where Brahmins bathe at dawn and worship the morning sun. Angry Brahmin at left finally won the battle by jerking out the oxen.

the warriors of the ruling caste. Others were created from his thigh, and they had the gifts of energy and enterprise. They became the Vaisyas, the farmers and traders. From his feet he created still others, the lowly Sudras, to be laborers and servants.

That is how one of the sages explained the origin of the caste or class system which has long been the basis of Hindu society. Everyone is born to a place in this system, and that place shapes his whole life.

The caste system is almost as complicated as a list of the gods of India, for there are many sub-castes—more than 3,000 of them. And below are millions of out-castes who have no caste rank at all. They are the untouchables—probably originally the descendants of local tribes conquered by the light-skinned invaders from the north who were the ancestors of modern Indians.

The constitution of the nation of India today outlaws "untouchability," and makes it a criminal offense to discriminate against anyone because of his caste, color or creed. But the caste system is still very strong, because of its basis in religion.

DHARMA OR CASTE DUTIES

Each caste has its own *dharma* or duties to perform. The priestly Brahmins have special religious duties. Though nowadays they usually have other jobs or professions, they must carry out prayer rituals three times a day. And they must spend part of their time teaching religion and conducting worship services for those of other castes.

The warrior caste is expected to show self-control, strength, gentleness and freedom from fear and hatred.

The farmers and traders know their duty is to work for service, not for special gain.

In former times, every boy in India knew just what his work would be when he grew up, because it was decided by his caste. The spread of education is breaking down caste barriers, insofar as choice of occupation is concerned. Today, an untouchable may, with education, become a leader of the nation. But members are still likely to marry within their own caste. And castes still have deep meaning in the Hindu world.

KARMA OR THE COSMIC LAW OF CAUSE AND EFFECT

The caste into which one is born is the result of one's past life, Hindus believe. One will be reborn in a future life in accordance with one's behavior in this life. This record of behavior through former lives is a man's *karma*. A man rises in caste through life after life—or through incarnation after reincarnation—as his *karma* shows a record of increasing virtue.

But higher caste carries greater responsibility, too. The misdeeds of a Brahmin are far more serious than those of an untouchable. A Brahmin who is greedy, for example, may theoretically drop as low as a pig in his next incarnation.

Only a holy man is beyond family, caste, even religious duties. He is cut off completely from the world and is one with God.

Women

No act is ever to be done according to her own will by a young girl, a young woman, or even by an old woman, though in their own houses. In her childhood a girl should be under the will of her father; in her youth, of her husband; her husband being dead, of her sons. . . . She must always be cheerful and clever in household business, with the furniture well cleaned, and with not a free hand in expenditure. . . . The good wife of a husband must never do anything disagreeable to him. . . . She must be till death subdued, intent, chaste. . . . Wife, son and slave, these three are said to be without property: whatever property they acquire is his to whom they belong.

—from the Ordinances of Manu

The untouchables, segregated from the main village, worship with sword and trident, symbols of the god Shiva. They do not use village temples.

LOVE OF ALL

Even the lowliest creatures
are a sacred part of life

Privileged monkeys, living in a temple of Hanuman the monkey god, are fed peanuts by priests.

Seeing God in everything, the Hindus have reverence for life in every form—trees and rivers, cows and even ants. This reverence is shown in the principle known as *ahimsa*. *Ahimsa* stands for nonviolence to animals as well as to humans. This is why most pious Hindus eat no meat. It would be against their religion to have an animal killed to provide them with food.

For a Hindu to eat beef is a sacrilege about equal to cannibalism. "All that kill . . . cows," the scriptures warn, "rot in hell for as many years as there are hairs on the body of the (slain) cow." Some Hindus bow deeply to all cows that they pass, and wealthy men endow places to take care of old and decrepit cows. "The cow is a poem of pity," wrote Mahatma Gandhi. "She is mother to millions of Indian mankind." Throughout history, Indians have used the cow for pulling plows, and for milk.

◄ *A festive face is painted on an elephant for Dewali holiday because Hindus like to have animals take part in their celebrations.*

Even insects are protected by *ahimsa*. A devout housewife will throw out crumbs as a gift of hospitality to the insects. On festival days she may make elaborate designs of wet rice flour before her doorway. These designs are good luck symbols that please the spirits who guard the doorway, but they also provide a banquet for the ants.

On holidays, good luck designs in wet rice powder are spread out before temple doorways.

HOW THE MONKEYS HELPED RAMA

Certain animals are treated with more than ordinary friendship. Thus special temples are dedicated to Hanuman, the monkey god, where monkeys live as privileged guests. This custom goes back to the ancient tale of Rama, the god Vishnu, visiting the earth in human form.

Rama's wife Sita had been stolen by the demon king Ravana. He carried her off to the island of Ceylon. It was Hanuman, monkey son of the wind god, who discovered her there. His monkeys built a bridge of their bodies across the waters to the island, and made it possible for Rama to rescue his wife. It is because of this assistance to a god that monkeys are still honored in India today.

WHY COWS ARE SACRED

It is rather startling at first in any Indian city to see traffic wait patiently while a cow ambles across the street. But no loyal Hindu would dream of bringing any harm to a cow, for they are all sacred animals.

Throughout India's long history, her people have depended upon cows and oxen for help of many sorts. Pulling plows and carts, providing milk for drink and food and dung cakes for fuel in the homes, the cow has been India's most valued domestic animal.

The Hindu affection for the cow is something special. The worship of a cow is said to give a married woman sons. And the feeding of any wandering cow is a worthy religious act.

When festival time comes in India—and there are many festivals scattered through the year—the animals are often given a part in the celebration. Temple elephants may be painted with fanciful designs. And cows are bathed and their heads decorated in patterns of yellow and red. For surely sacred animals should have a share in happy days.

A sacred cow lies down beside a dry riverbed, where a group of Hindus sit listening to a sage.

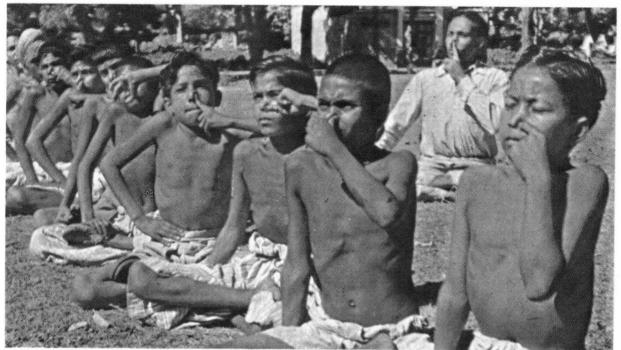

Breath control is taught to a group of young Hindus in School

A PATH TO BRAHMAN

Physical control through yoga leads to control
of the mind and the putting aside all desires

God may be reached by more than one path. For some, the way to God leads step by step through quiet days of work well done; for others, the path of the mystic beckons away from the busy world.

Nowhere else on earth does withdrawal from the world attract as many people as in India. Even small boys sometimes run away from home to become *sadhus*, "those who have renounced." The truly religious man, the Hindus say, "pants after God as a miser after gold."

The discipline of mind and body which leads to God is called *yoga*, the yoking of the mind to God. One who practices *yoga* is a *yogi*. *Yogis* are said to have such control over their bodies that some can stop their heartbeats for a minute and hold their breath for hours.

In the highest state, a meditating *yogi* cuts off all his senses: he does not hear or see or taste or feel or smell. Beyond good and evil, time and space, he is one with God.

THE TWICE BORN

Most Hindus, however, live out a more ordinary life. As children they are busy learning, especially the wisdom of their religion, which they must study and memorize by ear instead of reading in books.

The high point of a Hindu boy's childhood is his initiation into his caste. During the ceremony the boy sits near a sacrificial fire in the family courtyard. Beside him sits his *guru*, his religious teacher, who has prepared him for the day. The climax of the ceremony comes when the boy receives the sacred thread or cord from the *guru* and slips it over his head as his teacher prays for his strength, long life and wisdom in God. This is pictured on page 14.

27

A wandering sadhu, only 16, stops in the wilderness for a drink. His only possessions are a water pot and a trident. Hindus are supposed to feed all sadhus, but the custom is losing followers because so many lazy fellows who are not religious in spirit wander the countrysides posing as sadhus.

Withdrawn from world, this young sadhu sits and thinks in a cave in the foothills of the Himalaya mountains. He eats one meal a day, given by local charity.

"The Song of God"

Pleasure and pain, gain and loss, victory and defeat, are all one and the same. . . . Poise your mind in tranquillity. . . . You have the right to work, but for the work's sake only. You have no right to the fruits of work. Desire for the fruits of work must never be your motive in working. Never give way to laziness, either. . . .

Aspirants may find enlightenment by two different paths. For the contemplative is the path of knowledge; for the active is the path of selfless action. Freedom from activity is never achieved by abstaining from action. Nobody can become perfect by merely ceasing to act.

> *Action rightly renounced brings freedom:*
> *Action rightly performed brings freedom:*
> *Both are better*
> *Than mere shunning of action. . . .*
> *The wise see knowledge and action as one:*
> *They see truly.*
> *Take either path*
> *And thread it to the end:*
> *The end is the same. . . .*

The mind is restless, no doubt, and hard to subdue. But it can be brought under control by constant practice, and by the exercise of dispassion. Certainly, if a man has no control over his ego, he will find this yoga difficult to master. But a self-controlled man can master it, if he struggles hard, and uses the right means.

—from Bhagavad-Gita

Boys of all three of the higher castes go through this ceremony some time between the ages of seven and twelve. After it, they are called "twice born," for they have been born, first into life and now into the caste and a man's full religious life. Now the boy moves into the men's quarters of the home and joins the men in their daily worship.

A MAN'S RESPONSIBILITIES

For a young man, life is very full, with working for a living, marrying and raising a family. But he is expected to take time for his religious duties. And he looks forward to the day when his sons will be grown and can take over the management of the family. Then he can give his full time to devotion to God.

DEATH AND REBIRTH

Death is but a turning of the endless wheel of life

Life and Death

Life is transitory. So are the youth and wealth of a man. Wives, children, friends and relations are but passing shadows in life. Only virtue and good deeds endure. . . . The rest is but changeful like a wave of the ocean. Ah, what is the end of life? What does glory, fame or honor signify? Death with his attendants Day and Night is always traveling the world in the guise of Old Age, and is devouring all created beings. . . .

—from Garuda Purana

Moksha, the release from a long series of rebirths, is the goal of every Hindu. So the biggest event in his life is really his death.

When a Hindu thinks he is about to die, his first thought is to travel if possible to the holy city of Benares. If he can bathe in the sacred river Ganges, he will be freed of his sins.

If he cannot manage this, his friends will

Ashes of the dead, reverently carried from the pyres in cloth sacks, are scattered with flower petals into the Ganges at a holy spot near Allahabad.

Shrouded corpses, carried by mourners through the streets of Benares, are laid on a ghat. They will be burned on the pyre at left. Red shrouds are for wives; white for males, widows and unmarried girls.

gather with offerings to smooth his passage across the dark river between the land of the living and the realm of Yama, ruler of the dead.

The body will be burned, before sundown. If there is a stream near by, it will be burned on the *ghat* or waterfront stairway, and the ashes will be thrown into the river.

Only the bodies of the holiest of the holy men, the *sannyasi*, need not be burned. They have already been united with Brahman, it is felt, so their bodies are reverently dropped into the river, weighted down with stones. As the body sinks, the disciples blow on conch shells and chant hymns, celebrating another human soul's entering into union with God.

For others, death leads through a period in heaven or hell to rebirth in another body, another turn of life's wheel.

31

FESTIVALS

Hinduism is a religion full of life, color and emotion

Hinduism is stronger among the ordinary people of India than it has been for several centuries. One reason for this, at a time of problems like the present, is that Hinduism is a religion rich in life, color and emotion. Its goal is the soul's release from the world. But its festivals are lively and brilliant. There are gay holy days, temple ceremonies and marriage feasts. There are drums and cymbals, the blaze of perfumed fires and of countless candles. There are processions of gaily decked elephants.

For the world, says the Hindu, is God's joyous creation, his *lila*, his sport. And it should be enjoyed—so long as one remembers that the beginning and the end of all things is pure spirit or Brahman.

HINDU FESTIVALS

A widely observed festival is that which closes the Hindu year—Dewali, the Feast of Lights. It begins at dusk on the night of the new moon of Karttika (October-November). As darkness thickens, lights spring up all over the towns and villages, outlining paths and streets and doorways.

These small lamps are placed to frighten away demons. But Dewali lights may have more personal meaning, too. Each young girl makes a Dewali light of her own. The picture of young Gita Mehta in Jaipur, India, on page 13, shows her guarding the Dewali lamps. And if a girl lives near one of India's rivers, she sets her Dewali light afloat on a small raft in the dark-

◄ Left: *Purification by fire is also a feature of Durga Puja. Since evil begins in the mind, in thought, and is then done by the hands, this young aristocrat holds two flaming saucers, while a priest holds another on her head, to purify her.*

A dance for Durga Puja continues until the dancer, waving two incense pots, drops from exhaustion.

ness. If it stays alight as long as she can see it, good luck will be hers through the coming year.

The Hindu New Year is a time for both gaiety and serious prayer. All who can possibly afford to do so celebrate with new clothes, special feasts, fancy cakes and lights. But it is also a time to balance one's accounts, both business and religious. A good Hindu ends all quarrels and forgives all enemies as the New Year begins.

HONORING THE DIVINE MOTHER

One of the biggest and most elaborate of the festivals is the Durga Puja, held in the autumn. It honors the divine mother goddess, the wife of Shiva. She is known by a thousand names—Shakti, Durga, Kali, Parvati and many more. And she is worshiped in many different ways.

The giver of life can be cruel as well as tender. The mother goddess in the form of Kali is

33

Bloodthirsty aspect of the divine mother Shakti is the goddess Kali. Here, impersonated by a man, she bares her tusks and sticks out her long red tongue. The crown is made of peacock feathers.

goddess of epidemics and earthquakes, of floods and storms. So temple images of Kali are often bloodthirsty looking, and animals are sometimes killed as sacrifices to her, even today. Suffering, as the followers of Kali point out, is a very real part of life.

But there are also happier ways of honoring the mother goddess—with offerings before her image, with dancing, and with the lovely rite of purification by fire. As creator and giver of life, the Divine Mother is kindly, benevolent and smiling. She holds out her hands to all creatures, asking them to come to her as they would to their earthly mothers.

Different Paths to God

You see many stars at night in the sky but find them not when the sun rises; can you say that there are no stars in the heaven of day? So, O man! because you behold not God in the days of your ignorance, say not that there is no god. As one and the same material, water, is called by different names by different peoples, one calling it water, another calling it eau, a third aqua, and another pani, so the one Sat-chit-ananda, the everlasting-intelligent-bliss, is invoked by some as God, by some as Allah, by some as Jehovah, by some as Hari, and by others as Brahman. As one can ascend to the top of a house by means of a ladder or a bamboo or a staircase or a rope, so divers are the ways and means to approach God, and every religion in the world shows one of these ways. Different creeds are but different paths to reach the Almighty. . . .

Men weep rivers of tears because a son is not born to them; others wear away their hearts with sorrow because they cannot get riches. But how many . . . weep and sorrow because they have not seen God? He finds who seeks Him; he who with intense longing weeps for God has found God. Truly, I say unto thee, he who longs for Him, finds Him. Go and verify this in thine own life; try for three consecutive days with genuine earnestness and thou art sure to succeed. . . .

As many have merely heard of snow but not seen it, so many are the religious preachers who have read only in books about the attributes of God. . . . And as many have seen but not tasted it, so many are the religious teachers who have got only a glimpse of the divine glory, but have not understood its real essence. He . . . alone can describe God who has associated with Him in His different aspects, now as a servant of God, then as a friend of God, then as a lover of God, or as being absorbed in Him. . . . The sunlight is one and the same wherever it falls, but only bright surfaces like water, mirrors and polished metals can reflect it fully. So is the divine light. It falls equally and impartially on all hearts, but only the pure and clean hearts of the good and holy can fully reflect it.

—*from Shri Ramakrishna's Sayings*

THE PATH OF
BUDDHISM

THE PATH OF BUDDHISM

The Way of the Law

All that we are is the result of what we have thought: it is founded on our thoughts. . . . If a man speaks or acts with an evil thought, pain follows him. . . . Hatred does not cease by hatred at any time; hatred ceases by love. . . . Carpenters fashion wood; wise people fashion themselves.

—*from the* Dhammapada

From the island of Ceylon to the islands of Japan, and throughout large sections of the Asian mainland, hundreds of millions of people —perhaps as many as 500 million—believe in a gentle and peaceable religion called Buddhism.

It is based on the teachings of a man named Siddhartha Gautama, who lived in the 6th Century B.C. This was the time of Confucius in China, of some of the finest prophets whose teachings we find in the Bible's Old Testament. In this great age for religions, Gautama Buddha —Buddha means "the Enlightened One"—laid the foundation for one of the noblest structures of thought ever created by the human spirit.

The religion has been growing and changing, as religions do, through twenty-five centuries. As monks carried it from land to land, various countries gave the flavor of their own native beliefs to the Buddhism they absorbed. We shall see how some of these branches of the religion have developed. But first let us look at the life of the man who began it all.

◄ *Making a pilgrimage, disciples of Buddha climb this peak in Ceylon to honor the legendary footprints of Gautama. The peak is also sacred to the Hindus as Shiva's peak, to Moslems as Adam's Peak and to some Eastern Christians who link it with St. Thomas the Apostle.*

37

THE WAY TO ENLIGHTENMENT

*The life of Buddha and his teachings
form the basis of a religion vast and varied*

The young Gautama was brought up in princely luxury and splendor. Like other boys of fortunate family in his time, he delighted in sports. Archery was his favorite sport, and it was in an archery contest that he won the hand of his bride.

Now it seemed that all the good and beautiful things of life were in Gautama's hands. He had three palaces—one for the cold season, one for the hot months, one for the time of rains; he had servants to wait upon him, minstrels to play for him during the rainy months, a lovely young wife and an infant son.

But this pleasant existence, shut away from all the sorrows of the world, did not satisfy young Gautama.

His father, fearing an old prophecy that his son would retire to a religious life, ordered him never to leave his palaces. But Gautama, disobeying, rode out one day into the world.

There for the first time he saw human suffering. He saw a man in the feebleness of old age. He saw a sick man, a dead man and a religious Hindu who had renounced the world and starved himself to skin and bones.

Gautama returned to his palace. But he was troubled in his heart by the misery around him. He decided that he must go off, as was the custom among the Hindus, to learn for himself the truth of life.

For one moment he paused at his wife's door-way to gaze upon her and his son asleep. Then he turned his back upon his life of ease and family pleasures and went out into the world in the yellow robes of a wandering monk, begging for his bread.

This golden Buddha in Bangkok looks down upon yellow-robed monks gathered to confess their sins. Behind the image another larger Buddha looms. Both are in the position, with right hand pointing down, which Buddha is supposed to have taken during his meditation under the Bodhi Tree.

Buddha's Conversion

I was tenderly cared for, brothers. . . . At my father's home lotus pools were made for me—in one place for the blue lotus flowers, in one place for white lotus flowers, and in one place for red lotus flowers—blossoming for my sake. . . . Day and night a white umbrella was held over me, so that I might not be troubled by cold, heat, dust, chaff or dew. . . . Endowed, brothers, with such wealth, being nurtured with such delicacy, there came this thought: Truly the unenlightened worldling subject to old age, without escape from old age, when he sees another grown old, is oppressed, beset and sickened. I too am subject to old age and cannot escape it. . . .

While I thought thus, brothers, all pride of youth left me.

Truly the unenlightened worldling subject to sickness, without escape from sickness, when he sees another sick, is oppressed, beset and sickened. I too am subject to sickness and cannot escape it. . . .

While I thought thus, brothers, all pride in health left me.

Truly the unenlightened worldling subject to death, without escape from it, when he sees another dead, is oppressed, beset and sickened. I too am subject to death and cannot escape it. . . .

While I thought thus, brothers, all pride in life left me.

—from Anguttara-Nikaya

The sacred Bodhi Tree, a descendant of the one under which Buddha meditated and was enlightened, is still a place of pilgrimage. These pilgrims from Ceylon are wearing ceremonial white.

THE RIDDLE OF LIFE

Gautama at this time was a young man of 29. He had made up his mind to solve the riddle of life. The search took him six long years.

First he joined five Hindu holy men who believed the way to learn the truth was to starve the body. Gautama starved himself until, pressing his stomach, he could feel his backbone. But this taught him nothing. Soon he began to eat normally again, and the holy men left him in disgust.

That was one extreme. The other extreme, the life of pleasure and richness, he knew well. And it had left him hungry for the truth. So he decided to try the Middle Way.

He ate enough so that hunger did not occupy his thoughts. Then he sat down quietly under a tree—the sacred Bodhi tree.

For 49 days he meditated. In a vision he saw the armies of Mara, evil tempter of the world. They attacked him with storms, rain, rocks and blazing weapons. And Mara himself offered the wealth of the world if he would give up his

Nirvana, into which Gautama the Buddha entered at his death, is symbolized in this reclining statue of Buddha carved from the living rock in the famous Ajanta Caves in central India.

search for the truth. But Gautama sat unmoved. The armies of Mara fled.

After 49 days of meditation under the tree, Siddhartha Gautama achieved the enlightenment he was seeking, the answer to the riddle of life. Thereafter he was known as the Buddha or "the Enlightened One."

THE TEACHINGS OF BUDDHA

Buddha arose and made his way to the holy city of Benares. There, in a park outside the town, he met again the five holy men who had been his companions. To them he preached his first sermon on the meaning of life.

Thereafter, for 45 years, the Buddha traveled up and down northern India, preaching and making converts to his religion. At last, his body worn out by his labors, he fell sick and lay down to die. He gathered his disciples around him and gave them his last teachings. Then he passed on to the Nirvana which his religion describes as the goal of all men's strivings.

Returning Good for Evil

A foolish man, learning that the Buddha observed the principle of great love which commends the return of good for evil, came and abused him. The Buddha was silent, pitying his folly. When the man had finished his abuse, the Buddha asked him, saying, "Son, if a man declined to accept a present made to him, to whom would it belong?" And he answered, "In that case it would belong to the man who offered it."

"My son," said the Buddha, "I decline to accept thy abuse, and request thee to keep it thyself. Will it not be a source of misery to thee? . . . A wicked man who reproaches a virtuous one is like one who looks up and spits at heaven; the spit soils not the heaven, but comes back and defiles his own person." . . . The abuser went away ashamed, but he came again and took refuge in the Buddha.

—from The Sutra of Forty-two Sections

THE WHEEL OF
THE LAW

*The symbol of Buddhism is the wheel
whose spokes represent the Eightfold Path*

THE TRUTHS AND THE PATH

The kernel of Buddha's teaching lay in two great pronouncements. One has since been known throughout the Buddhist world as the Four Noble Truths. The other is the Noble Eightfold Path.

The Truths are these: 1. Suffering is universal. 2. The cause of suffering is craving, or selfish desire. 3. The cure for suffering is to rid oneself of cravings. 4. The way to be rid of craving is to follow the Noble Eightfold Path.

The steps of this Noble Eightfold Path are: 1. Right knowledge. 2. Right intention. 3. Right speech. 4. Right conduct. 5. Right means of livelihood. 6. Right effort. 7. Right mindfulness. 8. Right concentration.

Buddhism has two great schools of doctrine: Hinayana Buddhism, which is followed by southern Asians, and Mahayana Buddhism, which is followed in China, Japan, Korea, Tibet and Mongolia (*see map on page 48*). The Hinayana exalts individual austerity and salvation by personal example. The Mahayana stands for salvation by faith and good works.

For Buddhists in both these schools of doctrine, to practice all the virtues necessary to walk this noble eightfold path forms a pattern of self-discipline. A steady practice of that pattern in turn leads the individual Buddhist to good works and peace of mind.

To Buddhists who do their utmost to live up to all these rules through many successive lives, enlightment will come at last. Then, freed from all worldly desires, a man will be freed also of the round of rebirths. He will reach Nirvana.

THE HINDU ROOTS

This sounds much like the Hindu religion's round of births, for Buddha had been a Hindu. He accepted the age-old idea that all living beings go through a long cycle of birth, death and rebirth. He accepted the idea of *karma*, that good conduct or bad is rewarded in future incarnations. And that the world is a place of sorrow from which wise men should seek release by taming all worldly desires.

But there were some things in Hinduism which Buddha did not accept. He disapproved of the Hindus' caste distinctions. He believed that all men were equal in spiritual possibilities. He avoided Hinduism's fancy ritual.

WITHDRAWAL FROM THE WORLD

To practice Buddhism ideally one must be detached from the turmoil of life. That is why Buddhism has become a religion of many monasteries and almost countless monks. The monk lives a life of great simplicity. Most of his time is spent in meditation and teaching. He owns almost no property and is supposed to get his food by begging. As he wanders with his rice bowl he must not choose rich homes rather than poor ones from which to beg, and should eat whatever he receives.

Yellow-robed Buddhist monks usually go barefoot and carry begging bowls (here hidden under their garments). Besides robe and bowl a monk owns only a needle, a string of 108 beads which he counts as he meditates on the qualities of Buddha, a razor with which to shave his head and a filter with which to strain insects from his drinking water so he will not do harm to them. ▶

RENUNCIATION

CHILDREN LEARN BUDDHA'S MESSAGE

In many devout Buddhist families, notably in Burma where the pictures on these two pages were taken, boys learn of religion at a very early age. When he is about four years old, a boy becomes a monk for a short time.

This ceremony is considered even more important than a marriage or a funeral. Before it comes a feast to which the family's relatives and friends are invited. It is the most expensive and most solemn event in the life of a Buddhist family, especially in Burma. A special pavilion is built. Food, music and presents for the assisting monks are provided. Everyone, even visitors, acquires merit from the ceremony. This helps them approach their next incarnation with increased good *karma*.

At the beginning of the ceremony, the boy is dressed in princely robes to represent the boyhood of Gautama.

44

◄ Left: A feast for family and relatives precedes the ceremony in which youngsters are symbolically initiated into the life of monkhood.

THE STEPS OF THE CEREMONY

At the beginning of the ceremony, the boy is dressed in princely clothes. For he represents the noble young Gautama (as in the first picture at far left). Soon, however, the princely garments are removed. The child's elders impress upon him the vanity of worldliness. Then his head is shaved. This symbolizes Gautama's decision to forego the pleasures of the world.

Next the small boy is dressed in monk's robes and given a begging bowl. A Buddhist monk solemnly repeats with him the sacred Three Refuges: "I seek the refuge of the Buddha . . . of the law . . . of the order of monks." Then the boy goes to a monastery where he will get his first taste of the monkish life which is a Buddhist ideal.

In the robes of a monk, carrying a begging bowl, the small boy goes off to spend the night in a nearby monastery.

Princely garments are removed and the boy's head is shaved to represent Gautama's withdrawal from the world of pleasures.

Nirvana

That monk of wisdom here, devoid of desire and passion, attains to deathlessness, peace, the unchanging state of Nirvana. . . . The steadfast go out like this lamp. . . . Where no-thing is, where nothing is grasped, this is the Isle of No-Beyond. Nirvana do I call it—the utter extinction of aging and dying.

—*from* Suttanipata

Proverbs

Wise people become serene. . . . A man who has learned little grows old like an ox; his flesh grows, but his knowledge does not grow. . . . Those who are thoughtless are as if dead already.

ACTS OF MERIT

Hinayana Buddhists believe salvation depends on one's own right living

For Southern Buddhists, especially in Ceylon, Burma and Thailand, the Way of the Buddha is the basis of their religion. They try to follow his Noble Eightfold Path. They try to live by his Five Precepts: to abstain from taking life, from taking what is not given, from all illicit pleasures, from lying, from alcoholic beverages.

They believe that a long road stretches ahead of them, through many lives, deaths and re-births. The way to speed their travel along this road, toward Nirvana, is through building up a favorable *karma* through acts of merit.

Meditation is an act of merit. From early childhood they begin and close each day in quiet thought before the family altar. Shrines and temples are open every day for prayer and worship. Attending a religious ceremony is an act of merit. And there are others.

One which was popular in long-ago times and still is among the very wealthy is the building of stupas or pagodas. These are the domed or towerlike shrines found in cities and in the countryside throughout the Buddhist world.

These shrines are not intended to do homage to Gautama as a person or even as a god. He is thought of simply as a wonderful man who had a marvelous understanding of the mysteries of life. Offerings of food or flowers, pilgrimages, meditation, simply walking thoughtfully around a shrine or temple, helping to feed monks or to maintain a monastery—all these are acts of merit. All will help toward rebirth in a better life. Thus they represent steps on the ages-long road toward Nirvana.

Right: *The vast Shwe Dagon Pagoda in Rangoon has many separate shrines, each housing a relic or reminder of Gautama Buddha. Putting gold leaf on towers or sweeping pavement is act of merit.* ▶

46

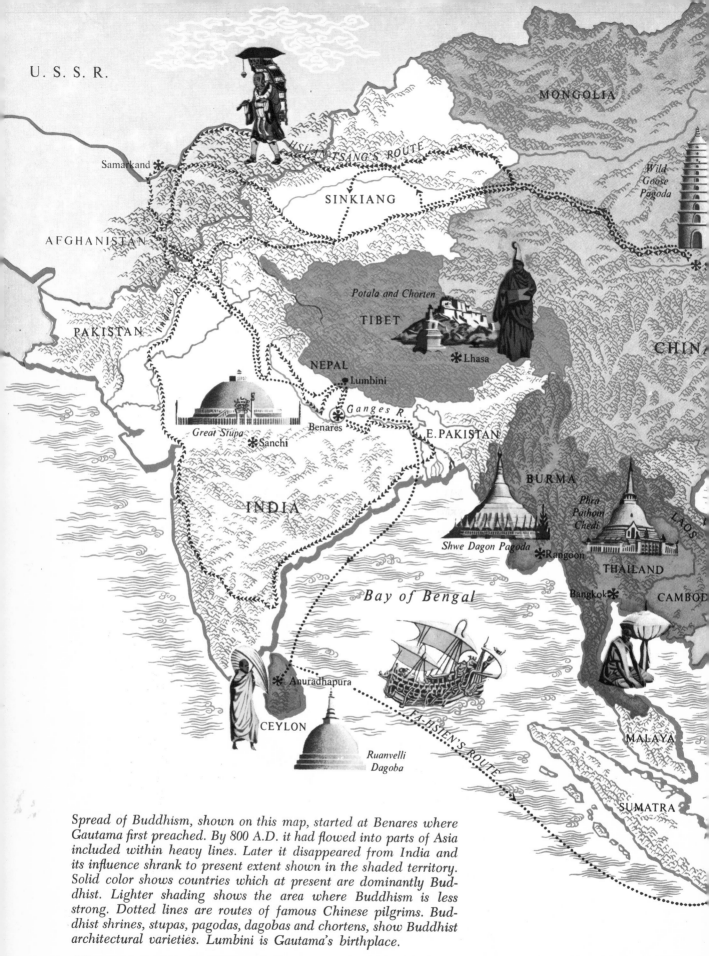

U.S.S.R.

MONGOLIA

Samarkand ✳

SINKIANG

Wild Goose Pagoda

HSÜAN-TSANG'S ROUTE

AFGHANISTAN

Potala and Chorten

TIBET

CHINA

PAKISTAN

NEPAL

Lumbini

✳ Lhasa

Ganges R.

Benares

E. PAKISTAN

Great Stupa

✳ Sanchi

INDIA

BURMA

Phra Pathom Chedi

LAOS

Shwe Dagon Pagoda

✳ Rangoon

THAILAND

Bay of Bengal

Bangkok ✳

CAMBOD

✳ Anuradhapura

MALAYA

FA-HSIEN'S ROUTE

CEYLON

Ruanvelli Dagoba

SUMATRA

Spread of Buddhism, shown on this map, started at Benares where Gautama first preached. By 800 A.D. it had flowed into parts of Asia included within heavy lines. Later it disappeared from India and its influence shrank to present extent shown in the shaded territory. Solid color shows countries which at present are dominantly Buddhist. Lighter shading shows the area where Buddhism is less strong. Dotted lines are routes of famous Chinese pilgrims. Buddhist shrines, stupas, pagodas, dagobas and chortens, show Buddhist architectural varieties. Lumbini is Gautama's birthplace.

48

THE SPREAD OF BUDDHISM

During the first 300 years after the death of Gautama, Buddhism spread throughout India and to Ceylon. In time, men of northern Asia, following the trade routes across the Himalayas, took news of the new religion of enlightenment back to China.

Buddhist monks made their way northward as missionaries, and Chinese pilgrims traveled in the opposite direction. Among these were two travelers whose journeys were as spectacular as that of Marco Polo. (Their routes are shown on the map.)

One, Fa-Hsien, left China in 399 A.D. and spent 15 years in India. The other traveling monk, Hsüan-Tsang, left China in 629 A.D., crossed the Gobi desert, spent 16 years in India and returned laden with books and manuscripts. He and his pupils translated much of Buddhist literature into Chinese. And the court of the great Tang dynasty emperor became filled with converts to Buddhism.

Also in the seventh century A.D., a great Japanese prince was converted to Buddhism and established it as a national religion.

Soon afterward a Buddhist monk crossed the mountains into Tibet. There he preached a peculiar form of the doctrine. It includes certain magical and mystical doctrines derived from Hinduism, and along with age-old sorcery and demonology long practiced in Tibet it makes up Tibetan Lamaism.

Wherever it went, Buddhism brought with it high ideals: tolerance, nonviolence, respect for the individuals in all walks of life, love of animals and of nature. But the type of Buddhism practiced in China, Japan and Tibet differed from that observed by the South Asian or Hinayana Buddhist.

49

BUDDHA OF INFINITE LIGHT

In Mahayana Buddhism, Buddha becomes a god of mercy, to whom the faithful can pray

From early times the type of Buddhism practiced in China, Japan, Korea and Mongolia differed from that of the South Asian Buddhists. About 200 years after Gautama's death, some of his followers gave a new interpretation to his teaching. On this, Mahayana Buddhism was founded.

In this doctrine it was said that Buddha's greatest virtue lay in his selfless devotion to others. For after he received his enlightenment he delayed his own entry to Nirvana for 45 years not to benefit himself but so as to share what he considered the secret of salvation with other human beings.

Where the ideal Buddhist of the Hinayana groups remained the *arhat*, or holy man who attained enlightenment for himself alone, the ideal Buddhist of the Mahayana became a *bodhisattva*, a saintly figure who has vowed not to enter Nirvana until the whole human race has achieved salvation with him.

The two ideals do not necessarily conflict. But their emphasis is quite different. The Hinayana stress is on each individual's master-ing himself, so that he may reach self-purification. In Hinayana thought Buddha is primarily human, while in Mahayana thought he is primarily divine. Since a Mahayana Buddhist can appeal for help to a godlike figure, who is a glorious redeemer, he can hope for salvation through his faith and devotion. For the average human being, this is not as hard as fully living up to the Hinayana ideal. So Mahayana doctrine appeals to the ordinary man.

Here the austere figure of Gautama is replaced by a radiant and merciful god known as the Amitabha Buddha or "Buddha of Infinite Light." Unlike Buddha himself, the Amitabha is not a man who once actually lived. He is instead a god to whom prayers can be offered. He lives in a heaven known as the "Great Western Paradise" or the "Pure Land" to which all good Buddhists can hope to go.

A goddess of compassion known in China as Kuan Yin (or Kwannon in Japan) also developed. She is said to guide the faithful to the promised land and is sometimes compared to the Catholic Madonna.

Kuan Yin, Goddess of Mercy, shown here in a Chinese statue, is known in Japan as Kwannon.

Paradise

". . . surrounded by radiant beams and brilliant jewels of untold price. In every direction the air resounds with harmonious tunes, the sky is full of radiance, large heavenly birds of paradise are flying to and fro. . . . (Amitabha) Buddha sits on a lotus seat like a gold mountain in the midst of all glories, surrounded by his saints."

This 42-foot figure of Amitabha Buddha, the "Daibatsu," sits in meditation at Kamakura, Japan. ▶

MANY SECTS, ONE RELIGION

Japan's 46 million Buddhists are divided among many sects but are devout and strong in their faith

Japanese Buddhists are devout. Nearly every town has a Buddhist temple, its solid walls often enclosing a park and playground and fish ponds as well as the temple. Inside the temple, worshipers offer their prayers and gifts of coins.

Like all Mahayana Buddhism, that of Japan is divided into numerous sects with variations in doctrine. Among these the Shin sect, with its many pageants and celebrations, is vastly popular. One of its ceremonies, a birthday celebration for Buddha (who is known to the Japanese as Sakyamuni), is shown on these two pages in pictures that were taken at a great temple in Kyoto.

Another favorite festival comes in midsummer. This is All Souls' Day or the Festival of the Lanterns. The shrines of the ancestors are decorated in all homes, and lanterns light the streets to guide the spirits home. At dusk small lantern-lighted boats bear the spirits away again.

Shin shu is Japan's most powerful Buddhist sect. It has the greatest number of temples, monks and teachers. It believes in the Amitabha Buddha and the madonna-like Kwannon. Its priests, unlike those of some other sects, are permitted to marry, and often pass on their office to their sons. Education and social service work make up an important part of its program.

Second largest, with nine million monks and laymen, is Zen, a sect of stern discipline. Plain living and long years of meditation are observed by its followers. Zen bears more resemblance to the austere Buddhism of southern Asia than it does to the other branches of northern Mahayana belief. Many scholars regard it as the noblest branch of Buddhism.

◄ Left: *Small Japanese girls wear heirloom costumes to honor Gautama as a child. They carry artificial lotus blossoms to this ceremony in the courtyard of Kyoto's Nishi Hongwanji temple.*

Gautama as a child, enshrined in pink flowers, is reverenced by a young Japanese boy carrying a tasseled rosary. After bowing before the small image, the boy will pick up a ladle and pour sweet tea on its head. For there is a Japanese legend which says that it rained tea on the day of Buddha's birth, and this is his birthday celebration.

ZEN,

A SEVERE FAITH

Meditation and simplicity are the keynotes of this group

Once during the lifetime of Buddha, a disciple brought him a golden flower and asked him to preach the secret of his doctrine. Gautama took the flower, held it aloft and looked at it in silence. His doctrine, he indicated, lay not in words but in profound contemplation.

From this came the doctrine of Zen, depending not upon books, preaching, or discussion, but upon years of disciplined meditation, which at last brings forth a flash of enlightenment.

Even such simple acts as tea drinking, gardening and the enjoyment of nature, according to Zen, contain the mystery of life and have religious significance.

Zen philosopher Shinichi Hisamatsu sits in meditation on his mat.

Tea ceremony, performed here by a Zen leader, is typical of the rituals which link religion to everyday life. Every move, every position, every tool is prescribed. Much of the simple eloquence and formality of Japanese art are inspired by Zen.

A Proverb

. . . Hatred does not cease by hatred ever; hatred ceases by love—this is an old rule.

—from the Dhammapada

Ethical Wisdom

All desires should be abandoned,
But if you cannot abandon them,
Let your desire be for salvation.
That is the cure for it. . . .
An excellent man, like precious metal,
Is in every way invariable;
A villain, like a scale,
Is always varying, upwards and downwards.

—from She-Rab Dong-Bu

BUDDHIST PRIEST

Keeper of the temple, a steady shepherd for his people

Conducting daily services in the temple, holding funeral services, offering comfort to the sick and teaching are duties of the Buddhist priests in Japan, such as this young married priest of the Shingon sect, who is on Naoshima island.

> ### Drought and Rainfall, A Parable of Buddha—
>
> *Brothers, there are these three persons found existing in the world. What three? The one who is like a drought, the one who rains locally, and the one who pours down everywhere: And how, brothers, is a person like a drought? Herein, brothers, a certain person is . . . no giver of food and drink, clothing and . . . bed, lodging and lights to . . . the wretched and needy beggars. And how, brothers, is a person like a local rainfall? In this case a person is a giver to some, but to others he gives not. . . . And how, brothers, does a person rain down everywhere? In this case a certain person gives to all. . . . So these are the three sorts of people found existing in the world.*
>
> —from Itivittuka

Traveling around his parish by boat and bicycle, a priest visits farmers, fishermen and other workers.

Sweeping the temple is a daily chore the Buddhist priest performs, though his wife helps him with many other duties.

Preparing a memorial tablet is one service of the priest. He gets no salary, but fees, donations and payments for instruction make up his income.

55

Tibetan Buddhism includes some demon worship. Here a masked Tibetan monk does a war dance.

THE PHILOSOPHY OF CHINA

THE PHILOSOPHY
OF CHINA

One day nearly 2,500 years ago the great Chinese sage Confucius was asked by a disciple, "Great teacher, tell us about the life after death."

Confucius replied, "We have not yet learned to know life. How can we know death?"

This is typical of the attitude of the Chinese toward the deepest mysteries of human existence. They have concerned themselves with the proper conduct of affairs and the attainment of happiness in the world here and now, rather than with the hereafter.

The Chinese social system—at least until Communism took over China (*see page 76*)—was based not on religion but on the ethical teachings of Confucius. The idea of God has not been very important to the Chinese; for them God is not so clearly defined a personality as he is to the Christian, the Jew and the Moslem.

THEIR EARLY RELIGION

In their early, primitive folk religion—3,000 years ago, several centuries before Confucius—the Chinese along the Yellow River worshiped their departed ancestors. And they showed great reverence to the mountains, rivers and soil. Each village built a mound of earth representing the fertility of the land. In the spring, with dancing and ceremonial songs the villagers gathered at this mound to ask the gods to grant good crops. Each autumn they gave thanks there for the harvest.

When the country grew in power and had an emperor—known as the Son of Heaven—it was at an open altar in the capital city that the emperor himself offered sacrifices to the heavenly spirits.

On the base of this ancient nature worship the Chinese have erected a complex structure of religion whose three soaring pillars are Confucianism, Buddhism and Taoism. The average Chinese has never considered himself solely a "Confucianist" or "Buddhist" or "Taoist." In 497 A.D. the court official Chang Jung was buried holding in his left hand the writings of Confucius and Lao Tzu, and in his right hand a Buddhist text. It is said he died "a typical Chinese."

Of the three, Buddhism is the most formalized religion. Confucianism is less a religion than a system of ethics. Taoism began as a form of mysticism taught by Lao Tzu. It has become a mixture of magic and religion; a Taoist priest invoking "water spirits" is shown on page 57. But Chinese literature is filled with references to "the harmony of the three religions . . . three roads to the same destination."

In the old Chinese idea, there is an organic and inseparable connection between man and nature. If man misbehaves, heaven is upset and earth does not prosper. As if to underline this interdependence, dead people in China to this day are buried beneath mounds like those that were once dedicated to the gifts of the soil. Moreover, both graves and houses must be in harmony with the rhythm of the universe. Otherwise, evil will befall their occupants.

It is this deep concern with the unity of man and nature that gives the religions of China both a sense of tradition and a joy that are matched by few other faiths on earth.

◀ *This guardian image was designed to frighten evil spirits. It stands outside a Chinese Buddhist temple near Peking. Buddhism introduced images to China.*

AN ETERNAL HARMONY

Both yin and yang are necessary to the order of the universe. Together they complete a harmony

In prehistoric times the Chinese saw in the splendor and terrors of nature the workings of good and evil powers. On the one hand they observed the order of the movements of the sun, the moon and stars, the predictable circling of seasons, the growth of plants, the flow of stately rivers. On the other hand they were confronted by the swift violence of floods and tempests, by the unpredictable disaster of droughts.

From these observations, ancient unknown philosophers worked out an explanation. There are in the universe, these sages said, two interacting forces or principles, the *yang* and the *yin*. Everything in the universe shows the interplay of these forces and possesses the characteristics of both in varying degrees.

Yang (red in the design) is the positive or masculine force. It is found in everything that is warm and bright, that is firm, dry and steadfast. It is the sunlight and fire, the sunny south side of a hill.

Yin (black in the design) is the negative or feminine force. It is found in everything cold and dark, everything soft, moist, mysterious, secret and changeable. It is shadow and water, the shade on the north side of a hill.

Heaven is mostly *yang*, earth is mostly *yin*. From them, all things have come into being.

Memorial birthday rites in honor of a saintly feminine ancestor are attended here by devout descendants. They are asking blessings on her from their patron goddess. On the table in the background they have placed offerings of incense, flowers, fruit and tea.

Everything in the universe contains both forces; at one time *yin* may be stronger, at another time *yang*. Think, for example, of wood, which is *yin*. Throw it into the fire and it changes to *yang*.

In the seasons there is a changing balance between *yin* and *yang* as the warm sun fades in power toward the year's end, then strengthens again through the spring.

And in each person's life, the changing balance of *yin* and *yang* brings now failure, again success, now flowering, again decay.

THE ORDER OF TAO

Yang and *yin* do not represent good and evil. In that this philosophy differs from others. Both *yang* and *yin* are necessary to the order of the universe. They are not always in conflict, like good and evil. When they are in harmony, they are always good.

And how can one assure this harmony? How can opposite forces be made to work together to produce the wonderful order of nature? The answer is: the source of all the order in the world is Tao.

Tao means "a way," "a road," or in a larger sense, "the way of nature," "the law of life." Even Heaven itself works through Tao. The gods act always in accordance with its way.

If everyone lived by the Tao, as the sage Lao Tzu described it, people would be natural and simple. No one would be ambitious for power. Everyone would show good fellowship and brotherly love. There would be no war.

61

FESTIVALS

*Ancient rites pay homage
to the spirit world*

For millions of Chinese, the important religious way of life is to recognize properly the power of the spirits that rule on land and sea and in the supernatural world. These nature spirits may be kindly (*shen*) or evil (*kuei*). Together they govern the fortunes and misfortunes of man.

From earliest times men have tried to make these spirits feel friendly through sacrifices and rites of thanksgiving. No marriage or birthday should be celebrated without considering the spirits, no building should be built nor any grave dug without consulting their whims.

For many centuries these spirits were offered real sacrifices. But the Chinese are practical people. They now use paper images for most of their sacrifices, or food which can later be eaten.

Painted entertainers amuse the gods as well as worshipers, it is thought, with their performances.

The Eternal Way

Man follows the laws of earth;
Earth follows the laws of heaven;
Heaven follows the laws of Tao;
Tao follows the laws of its own nature.

—from the Tao Te Ching

Proverbs

Leave all things to take their natural course
    and do not interfere. . . .
What is contrary to the Tao soon perishes.
The Way of Heaven is not to contend
    and yet to be able to conquer.

—from the Tao Te Ching

This boat for the gods is being made ready for its celestial passengers. At the end of the festival, the boat will be burned, returning the gods to heaven.

A traditional paper dragon in a Chinese New Year's parade is carried through the streets to the accompaniment of drums and firecrackers. Where it passes, evil spirits and misfortune are driven out. For the dragon represents the kindly powers of nature—rain and good harvests—prosperity and peace.

Even in Communist China the major festivals have still been permitted. New Year's is a time of family reunions shared with the ancestors, with feasting, firecrackers, gifts and offerings to Heaven and earth. The Dragon Boat Festival and the harvest-time festival are still observed. But many of the ancient ceremonies which gave Chinese religion color and pageantry and gaiety found in few other faiths on earth are disappearing in China today.

ANCESTORS

*To honor them is the heart
of Chinese faith*

In China no person is alone. He is but a link in the endless chain of his all-important family. When the Chinese use the word family, they include not only the living but the honored dead. Every man's home and property belong to the ancestors as well as to himself, for the fortunes of the living and the dead are woven together for all time.

In the home is a shrine where tablets honoring the ancestors are kept. In very poor homes they may be just bits of paper, but they are honored, as are the family graves. The dead are remembered in all family festivities, and especially on their own anniversaries. The more

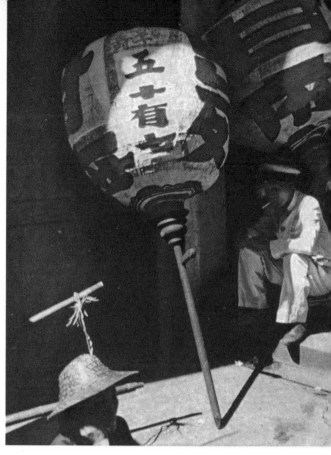

Lanterns at funeral give name of dead person.

Ancestors

Lin Fang asked for some principles in connection with ritual. The Master said, "A very big question. In ritual at large, it is a safe rule always to be too sparing rather than too lavish; and in the particular case of mourning-rites, they should be dictated by grief rather than fear."

—*from* Analects of Confucius

In this funeral procession the Taoist priests ride in pedicabs. 32 pallbearers carry the coffin from home to the graveyard at Tainan on Formosa.

64

The spring festival is a time for honoring the ancestors by cleaning graves, repainting headstones and weeding plots. Here a Chinese family in Malaya is making offerings of food and money for the spirits.

Character of Confucius

The Duke of She asked Tzu-lu about Confucius. Tzu-lu did not reply. The Master said, "Why did you not say, 'This is the character of the man: he is so intent upon making efforts to learn that he forgets his hunger, and is so happy in doing so that he forgets the bitterness of his lot and does not realize that old age is at hand.' "

—from the Analects of Confucius

honor paid to the spirits of the ancestors, the more likely they are to become kindly spirits. For their fate in the after-world depends not only on the kind of life they led on earth, but also on their being properly honored after death. Otherwise it is possible that they may even become demons.

In family life, the child first of all learns respect for his parents, for older generations in the family, for the ancestors and for older brothers. Family life teaches him the principles of right living with others. As he goes out into the world, he thinks of the whole nation as a kind of gigantic family. In the old days the emperor was looked upon as the kindly father of the nation, and the subjects were his children. And Confucius told his followers: "To serve those now dead as if they were living is the highest achievement of true filial piety."

The Best Saying

Tzu-Kung asked, saying, "Is there any single saying that one can act upon all day and every day?" The Master said, "Yes, it is the saying about altruism—'Never do to others what you would not like them to do to you.' "

—from the Analects of Confucius

Confucius on the Individual Path

The Master said, "Who expects to be able to go out of a house except by the door? How is it, then, that no one follows this Way of ours? Set your heart upon the Way, support yourself by its power, lean upon Goodness, seek distraction in the arts. To prefer the Way is better than only to know it. To delight in it is better than merely to prefer it."

—from the Analects of Confucius

THE TWO SAGES OF CHINA

Lao Tzu and Confucius shaped Chinese thought and character

Lao Tzu was born, according to tradition, on a farm in Honan province in 604 B.C. The name Lao Tzu means "Old Boy" or "the Eldest." Describing him, it means "The Old Master."

After a long career at the court of the emperor, Lao Tzu became disgusted and resigned his post. Then, according to legend, he decided to flee society for the unknown west.

Riding in a cart drawn by two black oxen, Lao Tzu came to a border outpost. There the gatekeeper recognized the sage and begged him to stay long enough to write down the main points of his philosophy.

Lao Tzu agreed, and in a few days he composed the Tao Tê Ching, the bible of Taoism. Then he vanished over the mountain pass, never to be seen again.

The teachings he left behind him were gentle and quiet. He was simple, humble, content to let the laws of nature carry him peacefully through life. For any use of force, he felt, was against Tao.

But from the start, Lao Tzu insisted that it was impossible to give his faith an exact name or description. His followers accordingly added to—and changed—his teaching, trying to make their lives happy and prosperous.

So as the centuries rolled by, the old nature spirits crept back into Taoism. The quiet meditation of Lao Tzu was replaced by all sorts of magical practices. The harmony of his gentle Way was jarred by old superstitious rites.

The philosopher Lao Tzu, father of Taoism, is pictured astride an ox, symbolizing spiritual strength. Red stamps are seals of picture's many owners.

Today the Old Master would scarcely recognize the religion which bears the name of his teaching. But here and there a lone man turns his back on the hubbub of civilization and goes off by himself to the mountains or the forests to live as a hermit and meditate on The Way.

MASTER K'UNG—CONFUCIUS

Confucius was born into a poor but aristocratic family in Shantung province in 551 B.C. His family name was K'ung. Confucius is the Latin form into which Jesuit missionaries translated K'ung Fu-tzu, which meant "Grand Master K'ung."

Confucius' descendant, K'ung Te-Cheng, is 77th in the line. His great ancestor's portrait hangs on the wall behind him.

> ### The Treasures of Lao Tzu
>
> *I have Three Treasures.*
> * Guard them and keep them safe.*
> * The first is Love.*
> *The second is Moderation. The third is,*
> * Never be the first in the world.*
> *Having Love, one will be courageous.*
> *Through Moderation, one has*
> * power to spare.*
> *Through not presuming to be the first in the world,*
> * one can develop one's talent and let it mature.*
> *If one forsakes love and courage,*
> * forsakes restraint and reserve power,*
> *Forsakes following behind and rushes in front,*
> * he is doomed!*
> *For love is victorious in attack*
> * and secure in defense.*
> *Heaven arms with love those*
> * it would not see destroyed.*
>
> *—from the* Tao Te Ching
>
> ### So Says Lao Tzu
>
> *Without going out of the door, one can know the whole world. Without peeping out of the window, one can see the Tao of heaven. The further one travels, the less one knows.*
>
> *—from the* Tao Te Ching

As a youth Confucius studied the history, poetry and music of ancient China. He wanted to be a statesman, and wandered unsuccessfully from state to state, offering his services. But it is as a teacher that he has left his stamp upon the Chinese people for 2,500 years.

Confucius insisted that he was "a transmitter, not a creator." Yet more than any other one man he has shaped China. In 479 B.C. he fell ill and went to bed muttering, "The wise man fades as does the plant." A week later he died.

Confucius agreed with Lao Tzu that the Tao represented the great law of life. "If a man in the morning embrace the Tao, then he may die the same evening without regret."

But to Confucius, following the true Way did not mean spending a lifetime musing over nature and the simple life. He set up practical rules for everyday living. From his teachings, which his followers lovingly recorded, has grown the lofty system of ethics by which China has lived.

Together, somewhat like *yang* and *yin*, the different teachings of these two great sages combine to form a harmony.

TEACHINGS OF CONFUCIUS

The keystone of Confucius' ethics lies in his Five Relationships: between ruler and subject, father and son, husband and wife, older brother and younger brother, older friend and younger friend.

These five relationships are essential to the social order, according to Confucius. The father must show love, the son filial piety or humility; the older brother must act with gentility, the younger with humility; the husband must treat his wife properly, and he may expect obedience in return; elders must show consideration, juniors respect; rulers must be kindly, subjects loyal in return.

Foremost of these is the dutiful respect of children for their parents. For it is on the firm foundation of the family that the whole of Chinese culture has rested ever since Confucius' day. In the centuries since his death, he has been awarded the same sacrifices as the sun and the moon, and ranked with Heaven and Earth—the highest objects of worship.

Confucius on Goodness

The Master said, "It is Goodness that gives to a neighborhood its beauty. One who is free to choose, yet does not prefer to dwell among the Good—how can he be accorded the name of wise? Is Goodness indeed so far away? If we really wanted Goodness, we should find that it was at our very side. Neither the scholar who has truly the heart of a scholar nor the man of good stock who has the qualities that belong to good stock, will ever seek life at the expense of Goodness, and it may be that he has to give his life in order to achieve Goodness. The Good man does not grieve that other people do not recog- nize his merits. His only anxiety is lest he should fail to recognize theirs. . . .

Chung-kung asked about Goodness. The Master said, "Behave when away from home as though you were in the presence of an important guest. Deal with the common people as if you were offici- ating at an important sacrifice. Never do to others what you would not like them to do to you. Then there will be no feelings of opposition to you, whether it is the affairs of a State you are handling, or the affairs of a family."

—from the Analects of Confucius

◄ *The teacher Confucius is shown in this painting seated on a dais, lecturing to his disciples. He had, according to tradition, 3,000 pupils. The painting illustrates the first of the 18 chapters of his* Classic of Filial Piety *which states, "The duty of children to their parents is the fountain whence all other virtues spring."*

This temple of Confucius in Peking was begun in the 13th Century. This arch opens into the Hall of Classics, containing 300 stone tablets on which are inscribed the Confucian classics.

CONFUCIANISM

*From a school of thought
came a state religion*

Confucius never pictured himself as the founder of a faith. His teachings actually had little to say about religion. He acknowledged the existence of spirits and approved of paying proper respects to both nature spirits and to ancestors. But beyond that he did not give much thought to the supernatural.

He turned his attention instead to giving rules for governing a country; for being a true gentleman and scholar (it was because of Confucius that scholars held positions of such importance in China); for being a true friend in time of need; and for being a proper member of any group in which one might find oneself.

As early as 195 B.C., though, an emperor visited Confucius' tomb and offered sacrifices. Soon his teachings were made the basis for the training of all government officials. From that time onward emperor after emperor tried to outdo his predecessors in honoring the name of Master K'ung.

Shrines were erected all over the empire, honoring him not as a god but as a sage and as an ideal. With passing centuries lofty titles were heaped upon him. At last he was actually raised to the rank of the gods.

After the Chinese empire ended, Confucianism was no longer a state religion, but his birthday is still a holiday observed by free Chinese and others who wish to honor the sage.

◄ *Confucius' birthday, his 2,505th, was celebrated in 1954 by these red-robed Korean students. Twice a year the emperor himself used to visit the great temple in Peking and chant: "Great art thou, O thou of perfect wisdom. Full is thy virtue, thy doctrine complete. Mortals have never known thy equal. All kings honor thee. Thine ordinances and laws have come down to us in glory. Filled with awe we clash our cymbals and strike our bells."*

Three Points

Tzu-ch'in questioned Po Yu (Confucius' son), saying, "As his son, you must after all surely have heard something different from what the rest of us hear." Po Yu replied, saying, "No. Once when he was standing alone, and I was hurrying past him across the courtyard, he said, 'Have you studied the Songs?' I replied, saying, 'No.' He said, 'If you do not study the Songs, you will find yourself at a loss in conversation.' So I retired and studied the Songs. Another day he was again standing alone, and as I hurried across the courtyard, he said, 'Have you studied the rituals?' I replied, saying, 'No.' He said, 'If you do not study the rituals, you will find yourself at a loss how to take your stand (on public occasions).' So I retired and studied the rituals. These two things I heard from him." Tzu-ch'in came away delighted, saying, "I asked about one point, but got information about three. I learnt about the Songs, about the rituals, and also learnt that a gentleman keeps his son at a distance."

—from the Analects of Confucius

True Worth

Tzu-lu said, "Is courage to be prized by a gentleman?" The Master said, "A gentleman gives the first place to Right. If a gentleman has courage but neglects Right, he becomes turbulent. If a small man has courage but neglects Right, he becomes a thief."

The Master said, "The gentleman can influence those who are above him; the small man can only influence those who are below him.

"The essence of the gentleman is that of wind; the essence of small people is that of grass. And when a wind passes over the grass, it cannot choose but bend.

"A gentleman in his dealings with the world has neither enmities nor affections, but wherever he sees Right, he ranges himself beside it. He does not mind not being in office; all he minds about is whether he has qualities that entitle him to office. He does not mind failing to get recognition; he is too busy doing the things that entitle him to recognition."

—from the Analects of Confucius

The Life of Confucius

The Master said, "At fifteen, I had set my heart upon learning. At thirty, I had formed my character. At forty, I no longer suffered from perplexities. At fifty, I knew what was the mandate of Heaven. At sixty, I heard it with docile ear. At seventy, I could follow the dictates of my own heart for what I desired no longer overstepped the boundaries of right."

The Master said, "Give me a few more years, a whole fifty in study, and I may be fairly free from error." He said, "I have never seen anyone whose desire to build up his moral power was as strong as his love of beauty."

Yen Hui said with a deep sigh, "The more I strain my gaze toward the Master's moral character, the higher it soars. The deeper I bore down into it, the harder it becomes. I see it in front, but suddenly it is behind. Step by step the Master skillfully lures one on. He has broadened me with culture, restrained me with ritual. Even if I wanted to stop, I could not. Just when I feel that I have exhausted every resource, something seems to rise up, standing out sharp and clear. Yet though I long to pursue it, I can find no way of getting to it at all."

—from the Analects of Confucius

This painting illustrating the **Classic of Filial Piety** *shows several Confucian virtues. The well-bred gentlemen bowing in the foreground are examples of "respectful deference" between friends. The group under the tree shows how people can live harmoniously if they have been educated in music and the dance, which Confucius valued highly. The peasant walking away from the sleeping figure (right) illustrates the virtue of "knowing what is wrong and forbidden," in this case napping in midday, it seems.*

On Knowledge

The Master said, "There may well be those who can do without knowledge, but I for my part am certainly not one of them. To hear much, pick out what is good and follow it, to see much and take due note of it (as I do), is the lower of the two kinds of knowledge. I for my part am not one of those who have innate knowledge (which is the higher sort). I am simply one of those who love the past and who is diligent in investigating it. Even when walking in a party of no more than three, I can always be certain of learning from those I am with. There will be good qualities that I can select for imitation and bad ones that will teach me what requires correction in myself...As for unwearying effort to learn and unflagging patience in teaching others, those are merits that I do not hesitate to claim . . . Where all around I see Nothing pretending to be Something, and Emptiness pretending to be Fullness, and Penury pretending to be Affluence, even a man of fixed principles will be hard to find."

—from the Analects of Confucius

The Secret of the Sage

The great rivers and seas became the Lords of
the Ravines by being good at keeping low.
That was how they became the Lords of the Ravines.
Therefore in order to be the chief among the people,
one must speak like their inferiors.
In order to be foremost among the people,
one must walk behind them.
Thus it is that the Sage stays above
and the people do not feel his weight;
Walks in front,
and the people do not wish him harm.
Then the people of the world
are glad to uphold him forever.
Because he does not contend,
no one in the world can contend against him. . . .
All the world says:
my teaching greatly resembles folly.
Because it is great, therefore it resembles folly.
If it did not resemble folly,
it would long ago have become petty indeed!

—from the Tao Te Ching

TAOISM

*How its high beliefs
were lost
in myths and magic*

The high philosophy of Lao Tzu was beyond the understanding of the ordinary Chinese. But he had said, "He who attains Tao is everlasting." That appealed to many. The teachings of Confucius had made old age a happy time of respect and comfort in China. So people longed for the secret of long life and some even hoped for earthly immortality. Now Taoist leaders began to supply all sorts of magical formulae for long life—from breathing exercises to diets of powdered dragon bones, moonbeams and mother of pearl.

Reception of the Immortals at the Court of Hsi Wang Mu is the title of the painting above. The Western Heaven in the Kunlun Mountains of Turkestan, ruled by the Western Queen Mother, Hsi Wang Mu, was one of the most important of the many paradises promised to Taoists by their religion. At the top of the picture the Queen Mother appears, receiving various hsien or immortals. Below her at left appear the best-known and best-loved characters in Taoist myths, the so-called Eight Immortals who had gained immortality for various acts of piety or heroism. The five old men at lower right may represent the five elements, metal, wood, water, fire and earth. The blue animal at lower left is a mythical Buddhist lion-dog; beside it (right) is the gentle chi-lin, the one-horned beast of happiness and good fortune. Above them eight more immortals disembark from a boat on the shore of Green Jade Lake, near where three female hsien talk together inside a cave.

A paper house is burned, along with other paper objects, to release a soul from purgatory. The Chinese long ago gave up making actual sacrifices and substituted paper imitations. A son of the dead man tends the fire.

THE DECLINE OF TAOISM

When Buddhism was brought into China in the first century A.D., it soon threatened the popularity of Taoism. For it brought to China for the first time a formal religion with priests, prayer, images and a vast array of gods.

Taoism responded by borrowing heavily from Buddhism. Soon it had priests, monasteries and organized worship. Buddhism had thirty-three different kinds of heaven, so Taoists soon came up with eighty-one. They took over many of the Buddhist gods, added others from the old folk religion, such as the Kitchen God, the God of Wealth, the City God. And they dedicated gods to stars, metals, and whatever occurred to them.

As the centuries rolled on, Taoism became so overloaded with fortune-telling, charm-selling and sorcery that as a faith it was meaningless.

CONFUCIUS AND MARX

China's traditional religions face a hard task

The Communists who now dominate China are opposed to all three of its traditional beliefs. Today the Chinese people have had to accept the severe Communist way of life, which rejects many of China's ancient practices. In the words of Lin Yutang, a modern Chinese philosopher:

"Whatever independent thinking there was came to a stop by the end of 1952. Both Confucian and Taoist ideas are now officially regarded as 'poison,' just as Christianity is regarded as dope for the poor. Confucian books are ignored, for all ancient books are supposed to contain 'poison.' Communist workers are replacing village elders. An elder or anyone else respected by the village community is a potential leader of the opposition and as such is liquidated.

"In every country, society lives by a set of moral values. In Christian countries, these virtues are represented by the Christian code. In China, they happen to be represented by Confucianism. Thus Communism has found it necessary to strike at the core of Confucian teachings by breaking up family loyalty. The denunciation of their parents by boys and girls of 13 and 14 has been systematically encouraged.

"But thoughts and ideas are somewhat like seeds. They have a way of lying dormant underground until a more favorable climate brings them again to life. As to when or how this will happen and when or how the Chinese people will return openly to Confucian ideals and the tolerance of Lao Tzu, that is a matter of international politics. But, as a Chinese, I hope that the triumph will come within my lifetime."

THE WORLD
OF ISLAM

THE WORLD OF ISLAM

"THERE IS NO GOD BUT ALLAH . . ."

Islam, the youngest of man's great universal religions, is also in many ways the simplest and most clear-cut. It honors a single, all-powerful God, who chose to speak through the prophet Mohammed. This God, whose Arabic name is Allah, is basically the God of Judaism and Christianity.

The Biblical prophets from Abraham to Christ are honored by Islam as prophets. But Mohammed was the last and greatest, the Seal of the Prophets. The Jewish Scriptures and the words of Jesus are respected, but the sayings of Mohammed, as preserved in the Koran and in other less sacred writings, represent to his followers the final and absolute expression of the will of God, who is one being, not a Trinity.

The Koran discusses man's fate in the hereafter, with its last judgment and its rewards and punishments—the beautiful green garden of Paradise, the terrors of Hell. But more important, the Koran gives clear directions for his behavior in this world. The true believer must honor his parents, help the poor, protect orphans, be honorable and just in all his dealings, avoid strong drink, pork and gambling, and be humble before Allah.

The word "Islam" means "submission" (to the will of God). A "Moslem" is "One who submits." Each true Moslem therefore is guided in his every daily act by the word of God.

◀ Left: *This ornate* mosque *outside of Teheran, the capital city of Iran, honors a Moslem saint who was a fourth generation descendant of Mohammed. It was built by admiring kings after the saint's supposed martyrdom in 861. Each year, some 300,000 pilgrims come to pray at the tomb and to touch the sacred fence that surrounds it.*

". . . AND MOHAMMED IS HIS PROPHET."

Mohammed was born in Mecca, according to tradition, in 570 A.D. At that time Mecca was a prosperous transfer point on the ancient spice route between India and Syria. Camel caravans brought traders of many lands and faiths. And pagan Arab tribes came in to make pilgrimages, worshiping at the city's numerous shrines.

Of all the shrines of Mecca, the most highly thought of was called the Kaaba (Cube). This rectangular structure contained various idols and, in one corner, a black meteorite which had streaked out of the heavens one night in the forgotten past.

Mohammed was born into the tribe which acted as custodians of the Kaaba. And his family's business was supplying drinking water to the pilgrims. So as a boy he had plenty of opportunity to observe the religious practices of both pilgrims and traders—Jews and Christians among them.

Mohammed early developed a distaste for the idol worship of the desert Arabs. And at the same time he acquired a growing respect for Jewish and Christian worship of one God. This idea made a deep impression upon the sensitive and thoughtful young man. Often he wandered into the hills to fast and meditate upon these things. Sometimes he was gone for days and nights at a time. On one such night the Archangel Gabriel appeared to him in a vision and cried, "Recite." Under this inspiration Mohammed recited what are believed to be the earliest verses in the Koran:

"In the name of Allah, the Beneficent, the Merciful! Read: In the name of the Lord who creates and has created man from a clot of

On this low hill, called the Mount of Mercy, Mohammed preached his farewell sermon, saying, "Know ye that every Moslem is a brother unto every other Moslem and that ye are now one brotherhood." Pilgrims still climb its sun-baked slopes as a part of their pilgrimage to Mecca. They are forbidden to wear head coverings, but may carry umbrellas.

blood. Read: And thy Lord is the Most Bountiful, who teaches by the pen, teaches man that which he did not know."

Overwhelmed with awe and terror, he rushed home to his wife, Khadija, a wise woman some years older than he. She believed at once that the vision was true, that he had been chosen to be the prophet of Allah, the true and only God. Then and always, Mohammed insisted that he was not divine himself, but merely a man chosen to be the spokesman of God.

The revelations from Gabriel continued. Sometimes even without his will, as he stood entranced in the city streets or beside the Kaaba, floods of rhythmic prose poured from his lips.

Since he spoke against the worship of idols, the priests of the Kaaba and the merchants of Mecca who depended on the pilgrim trade were outraged. They plotted against his life.

Mohammed fled Mecca in 622 for the friendlier city of Yathrib to the north. This was the Hegira (the Flight) from which all Moslem calendars are dated. (An A.H. date is A.D. minus 622.)

Yathrib was later renamed in his honor Madinat an-Nabi (City of the Prophet)—sometimes known as Medina. There Mohammed won quick success both as a religious leader and governor of the city.

His supporters soon launched a series of armed encounters, which ended in 630 when Mohammed entered Mecca in triumph and destroyed the idols in the Kaaba, leaving only the meteorite—the Black Stone. This shrine, he announced, was the sanctuary of Allah, the most holy spot in Islam. So ever since, Moslems at prayer, wherever in the world they may be, face toward Mecca as they kneel.

In the next two years Mohammed strengthened his position as a prophet and ruler in Arabia. He united many tribes into an army ready to conquer the world for Allah. So his death in 632 did not halt the growth of the new faith. It erupted into the world.

Generosity and Love

Allah is All-Embracing, All-Knowing. Those who spend their wealth for the cause of Allah and afterward make no reproach nor let injury follow that which they have spent, their reward is with their Lord, and there shall no fear come upon them, neither shall they grieve. A kind word with forgiveness is better than almsgiving followed by injury. Allah is Absolute, Merciful! O ye who believe! Do not render your almsgiving vain by injury and reproach, like him who spends his wealth only to be seen and believes not in Allah and the Last Day.

—the Koran

THE REVELATIONS OF ALLAH'S LAW
TO THE PROPHET

The Koran ("Reading") is the one sacred scripture of Islam. Moslems believe that all 114 of its chapters, called *suras*, came to Mohammed as revelations from God. All the words he received by revelation are held holy by Moslems, while his other remarks are preserved in the Hadith ("Tradition"), but are not thought to be holy. Daily reading and recitation of the Koran in all Moslem schools and mosques make it one of the world's most widely known books.

It is not certain that Mohammed could read or write, but almost from the start his followers took down what he recited, using "scraps of parchment and leather, tablets of stone, ribs of palm branches, camels' shoulderblades and ribs, pieces of board and the hearts of men." Soon after Mohammed died, these fragments were collected and made into the Koran.

No translation of the Koran has ever fully conveyed the eloquence or flavor of the original Arabic. And it is the Koran which still forms the foundation stone of life in all Moslem lands. The first sura, which appears on the next page, has been called the Lord's Prayer of Islam and "the essence of the Koran." It is an essential part of all Moslem worship, both public and private, and no solemn contract or transaction is considered to be complete unless it is recited.

Many of the Koran's stories are those of the Jewish-Christian Bible or tales of old Arabia. Many of its religious beliefs are the same as those of the faiths Mohammed admired. But it is a very great accomplishment indeed. For in the Koran one man put together a framework on which a whole people rose from idol worship to devotion to one spiritual God.

Charity

Whatever alms ye spend or vow ye vow, lo! Allah knoweth it. Wrongdoers have no helpers. If ye publish your almsgiving, it is well, but if you hide it and give it to the poor, it will be better for you, and will atone for some of your ill-deeds. Allah is informed of what ye do....

—*the* Koran

The Koran contains the law of Allah as given to Mohammed by the Archangel Gabriel. This copy was made in the Eighth Century, a hundred years or so after Mohammed's death.

The Unity

In the name of Allah, the Beneficent, the Merciful! Say: He is Allah, the One!
  Allah, the eternally Besought of all!
He begetteth not nor was begotten.
  And there is none comparable unto him.

—*the* Koran

(Mohammed said "The Unity" was equal in value to a third part of the entire Koran.)

THE FIVE PILLARS OF ISLAM

With no altars or images,
no organized priesthood or sacraments,
Islam is a noble yet simple religion
based on five "pillars,"
or principal acts of faith

A muezzin *calls the faithful to the* mosque.

Mohammed did not institute either an organized priesthood or any sacraments. He did prescribe several key observances which are known as the Five Pillars of Islam. They are:

1. FAITH IN ALLAH

Whoever proclaims from his heart—"La ilaha illa 'llah; muhammad rasulu'llah," ("There is no God but Allah; Mohammed is his messenger!")—is a Moslem. Some Arabs had long believed in Allah as the chief among many gods, ranking above all their idols. But Mohammed insisted that Allah was the one and only God. In the eyes of Moslems, even the Christian Trinity is faintly polytheistic.

2. PRAYER, FIVE TIMES A DAY

Since all the earth is Allah's, prayer may be offered wherever the hour finds you. But if possible something should mark off the prayer site as sacred. This tradition gave rise to the making of the beautiful prayer carpets of Islam. (One is pictured on page 77.)

The call to prayer is sounded, not by bells,

> ## The Lord's Prayer of Islam
>
> *In the name of Allah, the Beneficent, the Merciful!*
> *Praise be to Allah, Lord of the Worlds,*
> *the Beneficent, the Merciful,*
> *Ruler of the Day of Judgment,*
> *Thee alone we worship; Thee alone we ask for help.*
> *Show us the straight path,*
> *The path of those whom Thou hast favored;*
> *Not of those who have earned Thine anger*
> *nor of those who go astray.*
>
> *—the* Koran

which Mohammed did not like, but by the voice of a *muezzin* (see one calling above) calling from the minaret of a mosque. It is desirable for men and boys to pray sometimes in a mosque, first washing hands and feet in the fountain or pool provided (see facing page).

For the Friday noon prayer, men and boys are expected to go to the mosque if possible. There the Imam, an officer of the mosque, leads the worship and delivers a sermon. But most worship is individual.

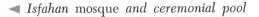
◀ *Isfahan* mosque *and ceremonial pool*

83

Women come out of their homes to join the public rejoicing in Cairo at the end of a Ramadan fast.

Women and girls may go to the mosque; in some a room or balcony is set aside for them. But most of the time they pray at home.

3. ALMSGIVING

A share of each believer's income should be given for the support of the mosque and the care of the poor. This has been essential because until recently most Moslem lands have had no organized charities. Now the Red Crescent, an

organization comparable to the Red Cross, is widening its influence.

4. KEEPING THE FAST OF RAMADAN

It was while meditating during the ninth month of the Moslem year, called Ramadan, that Mohammed is supposed to have received his first revelations. So the faithful, in commemoration of this, are commanded to fast from sunrise until sunset during the month

the dawn appears that a white thread may be distinguished from a black. Then keep the fast completely until night," says the Koran.

The fast of Ramadan is the most carefully observed of all religious duties by many Moslems. Not only must they refrain from all food and drink between dawn and dark, but they must not commit any unworthy act. One lie can make a day's fast meaningless.

Although the day is supposed to be spent in prayer and meditation, actually many people sleep. Trade and public affairs slow down. For those who must work, it is most difficult when Ramadan—which comes at a different time each year by the Western calendar—falls in the summer with its long, hot days.

But once the sunset gun has sounded, feasting begins. And at the end of Ramadan comes Little Bairam, a festival of good will and gift giving somewhat like Christmas in spirit.

During Ramadan, cannons announce beginning of each day's fast at dawn, its end at dusk. Here the sunset gun is fired in Cairo.

leading up to Mohammed's "Night of Power" when according to tradition Gabriel first told him of his mission.

On this "Night of Power," "the gates of Paradise are open, the gates of Hell shut, and the devils in chains."

Mohammed had known of fasting by ascetic Jews and early Christians. The Ramadan fast lasts an entire month, but only during the daylight hours. "Eat and drink until so much of

Some 70,000 pilgrims pitch their tents on the Plain of Arafat every year.

5. PILGRIMAGE TO MECCA

The rule that each true believer should make a *hadj* or pilgrimage to Mecca at least once in his lifetime has proved the great binding force of Moslems around the world.

No non-Moslems may make the pilgrimage or even enter Mecca. Pilgrims from every land approach the sacred city as members of the same family. All wear seamless white garments, abstain from shaving or cutting their hair, and do not harm any living thing, animal or vegetable. In their sense of common brotherhood, all barriers of race and class dissolve.

It is not enough merely to visit Mecca. Three main rituals are prescribed. The first, performed on arrival, is to run seven times around the Kaaba, as the crowd of pilgrims (*at right*) has done before these prayers. Starting at the Black Stone, the pilgrims run around the building three times quickly and four times slowly. On each circuit they pause to kiss the meteorite or, if the crowd is too great, they touch it with hand or stick.

Next comes the Lesser Pilgrimage, in which the pilgrims must trot seven times across the valley between the low hills Safa and Marwa. This commemorates Hagar's frantic search for water for her infant son, Ishmael. (Arabs consider themselves sons of Abraham through his son Ishmael as the Jews are sons of Abraham through Isaac.)

Finally comes the Greater Pilgrimage, to the Mount of Mercy in the Plain of Arafat (seen in the picture on page 80). There from noon to sunset the pilgrims "stand before God." This is the climactic ceremony. He who misses it has missed the *hadj*.

After leaving the plain, the pilgrims spend a night in the open (*see above*), then have a three-day feast. One final round of the Kaaba completes the pilgrimage—for a Moslem, the greatest earthly joy.

The Pilgrimage to Mecca

Perform the pilgrimage and the visit for Allah.... Observe your duty to Allah, and know that Allah is severe in punishment . . . and whoever is minded to perform the pilgrimage . . . (let him remember that) there is (to be) no lewdness nor abuse nor angry conversation on the pilgrimage. And whatsoever good ye do, Allah knows it. . . .

—the Koran

Pilgrims pray at the Kaaba, in Mecca. ▶

86

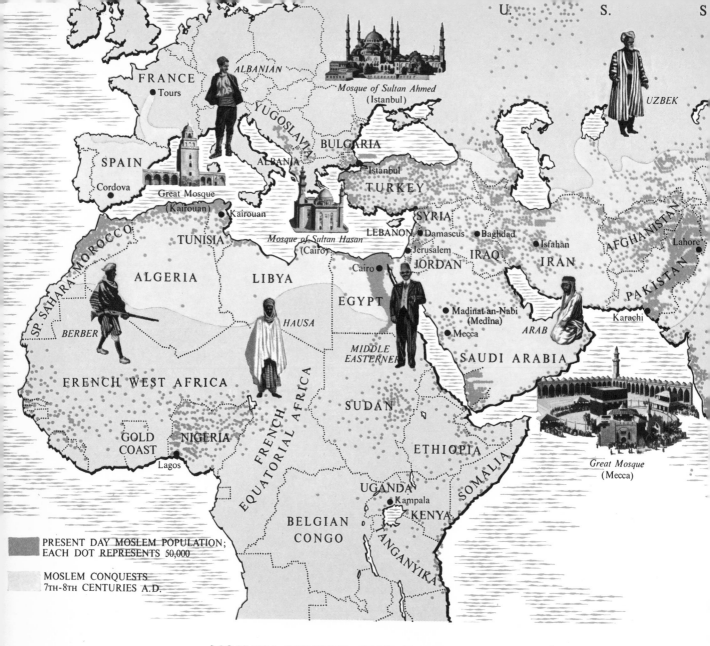

Map labels (clockwise/as shown):

U. S. S.

FRANCE
• Tours
ALBANIAN
Mosque of Sultan Ahmed
(Istanbul)
UZBEK
YUGOSLAVIA
BULGARIA
SPAIN
ALBANIA
• Cordova
Great Mosque
(Kairouan)
□ Istanbul
TURKEY
SYRIA
• Kairouan
Mosque of Sultan Hasan
(Cairo)
LEBANON • Damascus • Baghdad
• Isfahan
AFGHANISTAN
• Lahore
TUNISIA
• Jerusalem
IRAQ
IRAN
MOROCCO
Cairo •
JORDAN
SP. SAHARA
ALGERIA
LIBYA
EGYPT
PAKISTAN
• Karachi
BERBER
• Madinat an-Nabi
(Medina)
ARAB
HAUSA
• Mecca
FRENCH WEST AFRICA
MIDDLE
EASTERNER
SAUDI ARABIA
GOLD
COAST
NIGERIA
FRENCH EQUATORIAL AFRICA
SUDAN
• Lagos
Great Mosque
(Mecca)
ETHIOPIA
SOMALIA
UGANDA
• Kampala
KENYA
BELGIAN
CONGO
TANGANYIKA

PRESENT DAY MOSLEM POPULATION;
EACH DOT REPRESENTS 50,000

MOSLEM CONQUESTS
7TH-8TH CENTURIES A.D.

MOSLEM BELIEFS SPAN HALF THE GLOBE

In addition to the Five Pillars of Islam, the Koran gives rules for many other activities.

Believers are not to eat of carrion, blood or swine flesh. In both strong drink and games of chance "is great sin." Trading for profit is permitted, but lending money for interest is a sin. In marriage, though men are a degree above women, women may expect to be treated with kindness and justice. And if they are divorced they are to receive their dowry back—"Retain them in honor or release them in kindness." After the Day of Judgment, criminal transgressors "verily will burn in hell," while the righteous will enjoy the delights of heaven.

Islam was fortunate at Mohammed's death to be led by the three first Caliphs or "successors" to the Prophet. These were Abu Bakr, Omar and Othman. Under their skilled leadership—in warfare as in religion—it took less than twenty years for Islam to overrun in turn Syria, Iraq, Palestine, Egypt and the entire Persian Empire. All these nations fell into Moslem hands between the years 635 and 650 A.D.

So swiftly did Islam's onrushing armies advance that in the beginning they had time neither to convert nor to govern their new domains. There would be time enough for both in days of peace.

Indonesian Mosque

THE SPREAD OF ISLAM

FOR THE GLORY OF ALLAH

They contented themselves at first with collecting tribute. To all who paid this tribute they granted religious tolerance. Yet hordes of conquered subjects embraced the new faith that had come upon them so abruptly from the desert wastes.

Triumph piled on military triumph. The momentum of conquest carried the Arabs eastward to India, westward to the Atlantic, and across the Straits of Gibraltar into Spain, Portugal and France. At last in 732 they were halted at Tours by the Franks. This was a decisive battle, saving Europe for Christianity.

Still the energy of the young religion was not spent. It moved on into China and the islands of the Pacific.

Unlike most religions, which have grown slowly from remote beginnings, Islam came into being and spread with hurricane speed. Within little more than a century after the death of Mohammed, its dominions extended from Gibraltar to the Himalayas. Today its followers, at least 300 million strong, number nearly one seventh of the population, of the globe. From Morocco to the Malacca strait, Moslems profess the same beliefs, utter the same prayers, turn their eyes toward the same holy city. These things make Islam, for its diverse believers, the Kingdom of God on earth.

89

ISLAM'S THIRD CITY, JERUSALEM

Dome of the Rock viewed from Mount of Olives, over domes of Russian church, with city wall between.

Jerusalem is ranked only behind Mecca and Madinat an-Nabi (Medina) in sacredness.

Except for one century during the Crusades, when Christians occupied it, Jerusalem has been a Moslem city since the Caliph Omar conquered it in 638.

When Omar came in, he found that the site of the splendid temple of Solomon—and later the site of the temple of Herod the Great which Jesus knew—this sacred site had long been the city dump. With his own hands he helped clear away the refuse. And in 691 the Dome of the Rock was completed to shelter a spot

◀ *The sacred rock inside the Dome of the Rock. The hole in the foreground was formerly used to bear off the blood of animal sacrifices.*

long woven into Jewish, Christian and Islamic tradition.

Moslems believe that the great limestone outcropping within the mosque is the rock which angels visited before God created Adam, and that Noah's Ark sailed around it seven times. Here Abraham nearly sacrificed Isaac his son. Here all the great prophets from Elijah to Mohammed came to pray. From the rock Mohammed ascended to heaven on his famous night journey, and according to Moslems the angel Israfil will sound the last trumpet there on Judgment Day.

THE GOLDEN AGE OF ISLAM

From the Ninth to Eleventh Centuries a rich new culture developed in Moslem lands

A Sufi leader, advisor to a 17th Century Mogul ruler in India, tells his beads in splendor.

> ### The Devout
>
> . . . the likeness of those who spend their wealth in search of Allah's pleasure, and for the strengthening of their souls, is as the likeness of a garden on a height. The rainstorm smiteth it and it bringeth forth its fruit twofold.
>
> ### Children of the Lord
>
> Lo! those who believe (in that which is revealed unto thee, Mohammed) and those who are Jews, and Christians, and Sabaeans—whoever believeth in Allah and the Last Day and doeth right—surely their reward is with their Lord, and there shall be no fear come upon them, neither shall they grieve.
>
> —the Koran

The Ninth, Tenth and Eleventh Centuries were the golden age of Islam. Awakened by exposure to the Greco-Roman, Byzantine and Persian heritage, Islam evolved a brilliant culture of its own. The Caliphs soon united all their captured territory into a firm new empire, with a vizier in general command and an emir to govern each province.

Baghdad was made the capital in 762, and it soon was a center of science and learning. Art, philosophy and poetry flourished there and in other great cities of the Arab Empire. Mathematics and medicine advanced in a period when Europe was relatively backward. Moslem architects created masterworks like Cordova's mosque, begun in the Eighth Century.

◀ *The mosque of Cordova, in Spain, was turned into a Christian cathedral more than 500 years ago.*

Because Mohammed frowned on the making of images, painting never developed as an art in Islam, except in outlying areas, such as India, where this restriction was taken less seriously. But the new art of calligraphy—hand lettering—flourished. Korans were beautifully lettered by hand, and phrases from the scriptures were used as artistic decorations in carved wood, plaster, stone and even beaten gold.

Poetry too was a popular Islamic art form, especially in Persia. The Sufis (their name means "wool-weavers") were ascetics who from the Ninth Century onward tended to retire from the world, often into monasteries, to achieve a close, mystical union with God. They phrased their teachings in a lush poetry whose philosophical intent was clothed in the language of the earthly passions.

93

CUSTOMS AND SECTS IN ISLAM

Missionaries are spreading the Moslem faith and women are coming out of purdah and into the world

This woman doctor in Pakistan is a modern Moslem.

> ## Women
>
> And they (women) have rights similar to those (of men) over them in kindness, and men are a degree above them. . . . When ye have divorced women, and they have reached their term, then retain them in kindness or release them in kindness. Retain them not to their hurt so that ye transgress (the limits). He who doeth that hath wronged his soul.
>
> —the Koran

Despite all its vast successes, Islam has had many problems right from the beginning. In the early days differences arose over the question of Mohammed's successor. The Sunnis, the vast majority of Moslems today, believe his true successor was the first caliph elected after the Prophet's death. The largest minority sect, the Shiites, now some 20 million strong, hold that the succession came through Mohammed's family, and especially revere his grandson Husein. Islam has scores of other minority sects.

As Islam has spread around the world, the customs of conquered or converted people have also become entwined with practices ordained by the Koran. Thus the practice of keeping women secluded in their homes, or shrouded in heavy veils if they came out, is associated with the Moslem faith. Though by Western standards some Moslem customs seem backward, Mohammed himself advanced the status of women. Many of the rigorous restrictions on

Veiled women of Pakistan. The use of the veil (purdah) is losing followers in most Moslem lands.

Nigerian boys, as is the custom in a Moslem mission, chant aloud from scriptures.

women derive not from the Koran but from later interpreters of Moslem law. Mohammed did permit men to have four wives if they could treat them equally. Today, most Moslems can afford only one wife and family. Many daughters are being educated, some even for professions. Wives are more and more being allowed to come out into the world, since many liberal Moslems recognize that handicaps on women are a prime reason for the long stagnancy of Islamic life.

There are many other signs that Islam is now entering upon a new period of life and growth. In almost every nation across the Islamic world, Moslems are re-emphasizing their faith in various ways—politically, spiritually and culturally. Islam is adjusting to the forces of the modern world. Many leading Moslems argue that Islam should make every effort to revise its society from within and meet other civilizations on terms of equality and independence.

One example is a new Moslem emphasis on missions. The Ahmadiyya sect has an active missionary program; one of their mission schools in Africa is shown above. Islam is spreading rapidly in Africa.

The key question is how successfully Moslems can adjust their faith to the changes of time and history. The spiritual problems are the crucial ones. As Mohammed once told his followers, on returning from battle, "You have come back from the lesser to the greater struggle." They asked, "What is the greater struggle, O Messenger of God?" And he replied, "The struggle within."

Miniature tomb of Husein is admired by Shiites of Lucknow, India, on the anniversary of his death.

THE LAW
OF JUDAISM

THE LAW
OF JUDAISM

The heart of Judaism beats out in one sentence. This sentence has echoed through every civilization in the 3,000 years since Sinai. It is repeated by every devout Jew every morning and every evening of his life. It is the first prayer he learns as a child, and should be his last prayer before he dies. It is:

"*Shema Yisroel Adonoi Elohenu, Adonoi Echod* (Hear, O Israel, the Lord our God, the Lord is One.)"

These tremendous words were first spoken to the Jewish people by Moses as the spokesman of God. They make a sharp dividing line in the world's religions. For they created a new idea of God—the monotheistic belief that there is but one God of the Universe. Not only Judaism but Christianity and Islam rest on this idea of strict monotheism.

This God is a personal God, not in the sense that He has a body, but in that He enters the life of every man, with justice, anger and love.

He is a God of hope, for His followers believe the world is climbing toward a goal, the Kingdom of God. Life is not a burden to be escaped, but God's gift, to be lived fully according to His will. "Seek ye Me and life," He commanded in the words of the prophet Amos.

Judaism is a strongly earth-centered religion. It looks to an afterlife, but its practice is not so much to prepare man for the next world as to guide him in this. Its great concern is ethics— the attempt to find God's will in all things.

◄ *Reading the Torah, sacred scroll of the Law, in Hebrew is a proud accomplishment for a Jewish boy. Here the reader wears the cap or yarmelke in reverence to the Lord. He is reading to his father and grandfather, both wearing the tallit or prayer shawl. Pulling it over the head signifies a wish to commune with the Lord.*

This will of God is set down in the Torah, the heart of the Jewish religion. Torah, which means "law and teaching," stands for the five books of Moses—Genesis, Exodus, Leviticus, Numbers and Deuteronomy. But Torah also stands for all the Hebrew Scripture and for all the Law based on it.

In Judaism, as God is one, so is life. Every part of it is blessed. So the home must be a house of God, the table an altar, the market place an expression of justice.

The religious Jew moves through a round of blessings. On page 104, a Jewish woman blesses the Sabbath lights, and there are blessings for food and drink, for new clothes, for seeing any beautiful object.

The Books of Moses set down the Ten Commandments. But they also set down the right way to prepare food, to give to charity, to pay damages. *Mitzvah* in Hebrew means "commandment," but it also stands for "good deed." Judaism fully lived leads to a life of good deeds.

Prophecy of Peace

And it shall come to pass in the end of days, that the mountain of the Lord's house shall be established as the top of the mountains, and shall be exalted above the hills; and all nations shall flow unto it. And . . . out of Zion shall go forth the law, and the word of the Lord from Jerusalem. And He shall judge between the nations, and shall decide for many peoples; and they shall beat their swords into plowshares, and their spears into pruning hooks; nation shall not lift up sword against nation, neither shall they learn war any more.

—Isaiah 2

HERITAGE OF SINAI

The Law and the Prophets

Twelve-year-old Avrim Fink of Scranton, Pa., takes a Torah scroll out of the ark where it is kept in the synagogue.

In Judaism, religion and history are inseparable. The whole history of the Jews seems to be a continuous re-enactment of Exodus: bondage, liberation by God's grace, service to God as a result

Countless times, from Egypt to the Spanish Inquisition, from Babylon to Nazi Germany, the Jews were in bondage and on the point of being wiped out. Yet each time a remnant survived, while their oppressors with their armies and empires were drowned in the sea of history. That is the miracle of Judaism—its survival.

In Abraham's time the Jews were just a nomadic tribe wandering in the desert. Today there are an estimated 11.8 million Jews throughout the world—more than 5 million in the U.S. and 1.5 million in Israel. There are great differences among Jews but they are a people linked by a common history, a common language of prayer, a common and vast literature, and a sense of common destiny.

Jewish ritual is not very dramatic and its places of worship are without "graven images." Its real drama is its history, its greatest image an idea—the idea of the One Living God. When God elected them to be "The Chosen People," the Jews believe He gave them special responsibilities rather than privileges; He appointed Israel to be His suffering servant to bring His word to all peoples of the world. As Israel Zangwill put it: "The people of Christ has been the Christ of peoples." Jewish as well as some Christian theologians believe that the Jews' mission till the end of history is to bear witness against idolatry, against manmade gods, which are fashioned not only of stone and bronze, but also of false ideas.

Judaism sees man as a handful of dust—who also carries the divine spark. He is fashioned in the image of God, with freedom of choice. And at every moment of his life he is faced with the choice between good and evil. By loving God and trying to imitate Him, men also learn to love their fellow human beings.

The vision of Moses on Mount Sinai, when he received the Ten Commandments from God,

---

The Ten Commandments

I am the Lord thy God . . . Thou shalt have no other gods before Me. Thou shalt not make unto thee a graven image . . . Thou shalt not take the name of the Lord thy God in vain . . . Remember the sabbath day, to keep it holy . . . Honor thy father and thy mother. . . . Thou shalt not murder. Thou shalt not commit adultery. Thou shalt not steal. Thou shalt not bear false witness . . . Thou shalt not covet. . . .

—Exodus 20

This view of the country in which the recently famous Dead Sea Scrolls have been found suggests the wilderness through which the children of Israel wandered for forty years after being led by Moses out of slavery in the land of Egypt.

set a standard of righteousness for the Jewish people which has never been easy to maintain. During their first centuries after Moses, the Jews fought not only with foreign invaders but with their soul. For memories of less demanding gods kept rising up to tempt them.

They struggled continuously against human authority, too. After the reigns of David and Solomon, the realm was divided into two rival kingdoms, Israel in the north, Judah in the south. But out of these struggles came an unforgettable group of men—the prophets.

Repairing the Torah, this scribe in Jerusalem works on a handwritten scroll. A Torah must be handwritten according to strict rules, and always on parchment. Behind him are some 80,000 Torah fragments saved from European synagogues ruined by Nazis. These are preserved, for a worn Torah, since the name of God is written on it, may not be destroyed. It must be repaired or put aside.

The great age of prophecy came in the Eighth and Seventh Centuries B.C. Then the prophets stood behind the throne, in the Temple courtyard, outside the rich man's house. They cast a shadow over pomp and power, hurled their sturdy faith against mere empty forms of worship, protested against opulent living. They were imprisoned, stoned; but they could not be silenced. They were God's revolutionaries. Still, it was the prophets who added to the stern faith of Moses a sense of mercy.

The prophets showed clearly that Jehovah was not only an angry but a loving God. Hosea, through the story of the erring wife he forgave, taught the divine quality of forgiveness. Isaiah echoed the same message.

The prophets also vitally helped the Jews keep their identity. During the long captivity in Babylon, it was Ezekiel who insisted that they live by their own Law and ritual, to remain a nation. Many of the homeless, homesick Jews were tempted to accept the gods and the magic

A rabbi wearing a decorated prayer shawl blows the ram's horn, or shofar, *on Mount Zion in Jerusalem. The* shofar *calls people to prayer.*

of their captors. But the spirit of Ezekiel—a dogged devotion to the Law of the Torah—was later perpetuated by the scribes and the Pharisees. This continuing devotion has kept the Jewish tradition intact through many centuries of troubles.

The Roman Empire ruled Palestine for a century as a puppet kingdom under the Herods. But when the Jews continued to rebel, Roman armies in 70 A.D. destroyed the Temple (rebuilt after the Babylonian exile) and forbade Jews entry into Jerusalem except once a year.

There was no longer a Jewish state or a Jewish king. There was no one in power to be reminded of the living faith by the prophets. Now the place of the prophets as guardians of the nation was taken by the Law itself.

The Law was constantly being added to and brought up to date (as in the case of "an eye for an eye" which was softened to mean "some compensation must be given for damage"). In the Sixth Century A.D. all these oral laws, along with legends and sayings, were written down at last. They form the Talmud.

The Talmud became for the scattered Jews their homeland. After the Roman conquest of Jerusalem, the Jews were scattered throughout the Near East and Europe. They fared best in Spain during the centuries of Moslem rule. In Christian Europe they too often lived as despised strangers, often persecuted.

"Whenever the pagan within the Christian soul rises in revolt against the yoke of the cross, he vents his fury on the Jews," wrote an eminent Jewish teacher.

Throughout the Middle Ages, the Jews lived apart in ghettos in the cities of Europe, which was then divided into many small states. Here the Talmud was the center of their lives. It offered them escape into an imaginary world in which the Temple still stood—a world where the fields of Israel were still under the plow.

Life in the ghettos was not all bad. In them the Jews had a warm, closely knit community in which the old faith survived, unquestioned and intact.

But new developments came to shake that faith about 150 years ago, as strong nations arose in Europe, uniting the small states. These nations offered the Jews citizenship, but they demanded loyalty in return.

Now the Jews came out of the ghettos to mingle with the outside world. Some of their old customs began to seem burdensome. Some Jews modernized these customs and formed the Conservative and Reform congregations of today. Others have kept to the old customs, in Orthodox synagogues. And some, finding themselves in new societies not based firmly on religion, did not practice their faith.

Seeing nationalism growing strong all around them, the Jews too longed to have a nation of their own again. This movement, which brought about the state of Israel, is called Zionism.

The key fact about recent Jewish history is that the great majority of Jews have chosen to remain Jews. They still believe that they need both the Law and the prophets, a union of practice and spirit, to fulfill the injunction given them by Moses: "Love the Lord thy God with all thy heart, and with all thy soul, and with all thy might."

FAMILIES AND FESTIVALS

A home can be a fort of faith, a house of God

> *Hear, O Israel, the Lord our God, the Lord is One*
>
> *And thou shalt love the Lord thy God with all thy heart, and with all thy soul, and with all thy might. And these words, which I command thee this day, shall be upon thy heart, and thou shalt teach them diligently unto thy children, and shalt talk of them when thou sittest in thy house, and when thou walkest by the way, and when thou liest down, and when thou risest up. And thou shalt bind them for a sign upon thy hand, and they shall be for frontlets between thine eyes. And thou shalt write them upon the doorposts of thy house, and upon thy gates. . . . And thou shalt remember all the way which the Lord thy God hath led thee . . . that He might make thee know that man doth not live by bread only, but by every thing that proceedeth out of the mouth of the Lord doth man live."*
>
> —Deuteronomy 6, 8

A JEWISH HOME

At the door of many a devout Jewish home hangs a small box called the *mezuzah* (meaning doorpost) which holds a bit of parchment with 15 verses from Scripture. Often, as members of the family come and go, they kiss the *mezuzah*. It proclaims that the house is Jewish. It also marks the fact that in the Jewish faith the home is equal to the synagogue as a house of God.

To raise a family is a sacred duty to Jews. And it is through family loyalty that they express loyalty to Judaism.

Every meal is an opportunity for expressing gratitude to God. In an Orthodox home especially, all daily life is touched by religion.

> *Happy is the man . . . (whose) delight is in the law of the Lord; and in His law doth he meditate day and night . . .*
>
> —Psalm 1

Jewish mother says blessing over Sabbath candles.

With a sip of wine, this father leads his family in a ceremony at the Sabbath meal of a Reform Jewish family at Cleveland, Ohio. The Sabbath is considered a special blessing from God to his people.

For example, the Mosaic dietary laws are strictly obeyed. Dishes for meat may not be used for dairy foods. Pork and shellfish are forbidden, and all meat must have been quickly and neatly slaughtered so as to prevent too much blood from staying in the flesh.

> *And God blessed the seventh day, and hallowed it: because in it He rested from all His work. . . .*
>
> —Genesis 2

THE BLESSED SABBATH

The height of the family ritual comes on the Sabbath. Rabbis have described it as a foretaste of the world to come. This day of rest is a unique gift of God, which is celebrated with special food, song, and release from work.

Orthodox Jews not only do not work on the Sabbath; they refuse to travel, to use the phone, write, touch money or pose for pictures.

Many members of the Conservative movement relax these prohibitions somewhat. Reform Jews have generally abandoned them. But the Sabbath, beginning at dusk on Friday and continuing until dusk on Saturday, is honored in every devout Jewish home.

At dusk on Friday the woman of the house, with her husband and children grouped about her, lights the traditional candles with the blessing: "Blessed art Thou, O Lord our God, King of the Universe, Who hast sanctified us by Thy laws and commanded us to kindle the Sabbath light." Then the father blesses the wine with a prayer. The prayer concluded, everyone sips the wine—"praising God with this symbol of joy"—and the father slices the Sabbath loaf. Thus the Lord's day, a time for spiritual refreshment, for peace, rest and family reunion, begins.

On the Sabbath evening, Conservative and Reform families will go to synagogue after dinner. They will follow worship with an hour of sociability in the temple's meeting hall.

Evening blessing is delivered in Hebrew and English in this Reform synagogue service.

In an Orthodox family, the head of the house will have gone to synagogue before dinner. The main Orthodox service is on Saturday morning; the Orthodox and most Conservatives attend still another service on Saturday afternoon.

In Orthodox synagogues, men and women sit separately at worship services, and the Hebrew language predominates at worship. If such restrictions as these and the strict dietary laws seem to make life difficult in the modern-day world, Orthodox Jews answer that the Law came directly from God to Moses and cannot be changed. Even the Talmud was divinely guided, they say.

Conservatives attempt to make the Law fit modern life. The Talmud, they feel, was a product of its age and may be revised by a later age. Men and women usually sit together at their services and an organ and choir are permitted.

The Reform movement has, like the Conservatives, about a million members as against two millions for the Orthodox. Reform Jews feel that the principles of Judaism are more important than its practices. The practices, they

feel, are designed to dramatize the principles and ideals. Hence customs and practices can change.

Most Reform members do not observe the dietary laws, which they consider unnecessary with modern sanitation. They do not follow Sabbath restrictions, which seem impractical. They reject skull caps, prayer boxes and prayer shawls as being unnecessary.

They use English as well as Hebrew in worship, believing that it is important for the worshipers to understand the service. Men and women sit together, and music is used.

The Jews have an old saying: "More than Israel kept the Sabbath, the Sabbath kept Israel." The same might be said of the annual holy days. If each Jewish family is a brick in the structure of the Jewish faith, then the holy days are the mortar that keeps the bricks together. Even those Jewish families which seldom practice their religion do usually observe the important festivals.

Right: *Confirmation for boys (in blue) and girls (in white) at 15 is an innovation of which Reform movement is proud.* ►

106

Spinning the dreidel, *a four-sided top, is a Hannukkah game. These boys of Providence, R. I., are playing on a mosaic pavement in front of their synagogue which tells the Hannukkah story in pictures.*

The most solemn of these days are Rosh Hashanah and Yom Kippur (*see pp.* 114–115). Next in importance is Passover (*see page* 111).

All Jewish families, whatever their branch, seize on most holidays as opportunities to acquaint their children with Jewish history and philosophy through games and gaiety. Thus Purim is a time for children to dress up and act out the story of Queen Esther, who rescued the Jews from a wicked plot. Shabuot, Feast of the First Fruits, and Succoth, an eight-day autumn thanksgiving festival, let children undertake gay projects.

Hannukkah, the Feast of Lights (November or December), celebrates a long-ago victory of Judas Maccabaeus over the Syrians and the rekindling of the Temple light. It also shows the remarkable adaptability of Judaism and the connection of family to faith. Until about 1900,

Hannukkah was a relatively unimportant festival. But it falls close to Christmas. So Jewish families, especially in the Reform movement, have made more of it for their children. There is a moving ceremony of lighting the Hannukkah candles, and families often provide a gift for each child on each of the festival's eight nights.

Beyond the holidays, family ritual follows the cycle of life. On the eighth day after a male child is born, he is circumcised to recall God's covenant with Abraham. At 13, a boy assumes all adult religious duties.

A mother leads her rabbi husband and sons in Hannukkah singing. Their favorite song is the Jewish hymn "Rock of Ages" (not the same as the Christian hymn of the same name) but they also sing "Hannukkah, O Hannukkah" and "I Have a Little Dreidel." On the table is the menorah, *one more candle of which is lit each night of the festival.* ▶

*Blessing the bridal pair, the rabbi offers them wine which they
will sip to show they will share whatever fate may bring them.*

But a family's day of triumph is a wedding. An Orthodox wedding, like the one pictured above, includes formal questions and ceremonial sips of wine, to show that the young couple will share whatever fate brings. At the end of the service a glass is broken to recall the destruction of Jerusalem by Rome in 70 A.D.

Marriage is sacred to Jews. Divorce is permitted, but the husband, master of the house, is instructed to honor his wife more than himself, for she is mother and keeper of the home and, says the Talmud, "God counts her tears."

PASSOVER

The ancient ritual reminds Jews of their deliverance from Egypt

Baking matzot *in Jerusalem.*

"Why is this night different from all other nights?" asks the youngest child.

"We were slaves unto Pharaoh in Egypt and the Eternal our God led us from there with a mighty hand," answers an elder.

With this formal exchange between the head of the family and the youngest son, the services of Passover start.

Passover joyously recalls the Jews' deliverance from Egypt and the great Exodus which led them to Mount Sinai. But it also reminds them of other times of bondage and exile.

The name derives from the last of the ten plagues, in which God smote the eldest son of each household of the Egyptians but "passed over" the homes of the Israelites, marked with the blood of a lamb. Since they had to leave their homes in Egypt without even letting their bread rise, only unleavened bread (matzot) is eaten at this time.

A special housecleaning precedes the Passover, to rid the house of leaven. This sort of preparation for the holidays is considered an important part of the enjoyment.

After sundown the evening before the Passover, the whole family makes a final search of the house for any leaven which might have been overlooked in the housecleaning. The search is carried on in silence and by candlelight. And the children customarily find a few crumbs which the mother has hidden for them.

Special Passover dishes are used, if the family can afford them, for the ceremonial meal called the Seder. Prayers and food requirements for this meal are given in detail in one of the books of Scripture. The dishes served have special meanings. For example, *matzot* stand for the "bread of affliction." *Haroset*, a paste of apples and nuts, stands for the mortar used by the Jews as they labored for the Pharaohs.

The last *matzah* is usually hidden and searched for by a child amid much merriment. Since some Jews believe that Elijah will announce the coming of the Messiah on a Passover, they put out a glass of wine for the prophet and leave the door open for him.

The First Passover

And the Lord spoke unto Moses and Aaron [Moses' brother] in the land of Egypt, saying: ". . . . And they shall take of the blood [of the lamb], and put it on the two side posts and on the lintel, upon the houses wherein they shall eat the flesh . . ., with bitter herbs they shall eat it . . . and ye shall eat it in haste—it is the Lord's passover.

For I will go through the land of Egypt in that night, and will smite all the first-born in the land of Egypt. . . . I will pass over you. . . . And this day shall be unto you for a memorial, and ye shall keep it a feast to the Lord, . . . for ever."

—Exodus 12

Abraham

And the Lord appeared unto Abram, and said: "Unto thy seed will I give this land . . . I am thy shield." . . . And Abram said: "O Lord God, what wilt Thou give me, seeing I go hence childless?" . . . And He brought him forth abroad, and said: "Look now toward heaven, and count the stars . . . So shall thy seed be. . . . I am God Almighty; walk before Me, and be thou whole-hearted . . . Neither shall thy name any more be called Abram, but thy name shall be Abraham; for the father of a multitude of nations have I made thee . . . This is My covenant, which ye shall keep, between Me and you and thy seed after thee; every male among you shall be circumcised . . . He that is eight days old shall be circumcised among you . . . And the uncircumcised male . . . shall be cut off from his people; he hath broken My covenant." . . .

And it came to pass after these things that God did prove Abraham, and said: ". . . Take now thy son, thine only son, whom thou lovest, even Isaac . . . and offer him there for a burnt offering." . . . And Abraham built the altar there, and took the knife to slay his son. And the angel of the Lord called unto him out of heaven, and said: " '. . . Lay not thy hand upon the lad.' " . . . " 'By myself have I sworn,' saith the Lord, 'because thou hast done this thing, and hast not withheld thy son, thine only son, that in blessing I will bless thee . . . and in thy seed shall all the nations of the earth be blessed; because thou hast hearkened to My voice.' "

—Genesis 12-22

Purim celebrates with costumes and fun Queen Esther's rescue of the Jewish people.

The earth is the Lord's, and the fulness thereof; the world, and they that dwell therein.

—Psalm 24

(The Psalms, traditionally attributed to King David, have been called "the immortal song book of the human heart." One of the best loved follows on the next page.)

The ritual of offering to God the first spring grain at Passover is observed here by members of a collective farm near Herzelia in Israel. Here the festival is celebrated as a historic holiday.

The Lord is my shepherd; I shall not want. He maketh me to lie down in green pastures; He leadeth me beside the still waters. He restoreth my soul; He guideth me in straight paths for His name's sake. Yea, though I walk through the valley of the shadow of death, I will fear no evil, for Thou art with me; Thy rod and Thy staff, they comfort me. Thou preparest a table before me in the presence of mine enemies; Thou hast anointed my head with oil; my cup runneth over. Surely goodness and mercy shall follow me all the days of my life; and I shall dwell in the house of the Lord for ever.

—Psalm 23

THE HIGH HOLY DAYS

A time of repentance and soul-searching and of return to God

The holiest days of the Jewish year are Rosh Hashanah (the Jewish New Year, in September or October) and Yom Kippur, the Day of Atonement. Together, they form a ten-day period of repentance, soul-searching and return to God. On these two most solemn days, many Jewish business and professional men shut down their establishments and offices completely.

New Year's Day represents the Day of Creation; to honor it the *shofar* is blown—a trumpet of ram's horn which will blow on Judgment Day. It is also the day God passes judgment, in the Book of Life, on each person's actions.

God's Way

And what doth the Lord require of thee, but to do justly, and to love mercy, and to walk humbly with thy God?

—Micah 6

◀ *On the synagogue table (left) are the Torah scroll, its wrapper and the bell-hung, crown-shaped cap which fits over the upper end of a roller. Behind the rabbi is the Ark of the Covenant, with Hebrew letters above it spelling Shaddai (the Almighty).*

Gathered in this Israel synagogue for non-European Jews are elders from Bukhara in U.S.S.R., Yemen, Morocco, Afghanistan and Israel. No service is being held, but the elders are reading the Talmud, as they have done many times, for to Orthodox Jews it is an eternal source of instruction.

YOM KIPPUR

Yom Kippur is the Day of Atonement. It is observed with a 24-hour fast, from sundown to sundown. And even people who do not often attend the synagogue try to be present for the special holiday services.

Children are not expected to keep the 24-hour fast, but it is a matter of pride to fast for at least one meal, and, as they grow older, for more. To take part in the services of the High Holy Days is a high privilege as well as a duty.

Simchath Torah, or Rejoicing in the Law, marks the end of the yearly cycle of Torah reading in the synagogues. It is celebrated in September or October. Between services, in many Orthodox synagogues, elders of the congregation gather to read from the ancient books of law for their own instruction.

115

A Conservative rabbi teaches a student in a book-lined study that shows Jewish love of learning.

EDUCATION *For a good life*

Educating children to live by God's laws is one of the prime duties of Jewish parents. Children are welcomed into the congregation at birth. Boy babies are circumcised at eight days. Girl babies are welcomed with a prayer.

Children of the small, superorthodox group called Hassidim *start learning the Torah at 3 and 4 years.*

Most Jewish children in the United States, whether their families are of Orthodox, Conservative or Reform faith, learn some Hebrew. The letters of the Hebrew alphabet, as indicated in the picture to the right, are quite different from those of our alphabet; Hebrew is also read and written from right to left.

Whenever possible, children learn to read and write in Hebrew the great sentence: "Hear, O Israel, the Lord our God, the Lord is One." But even before this, in the home, they have begun to feel the atmosphere of worship in the Sabbath ceremonies, and to take part in many of the Jewish holidays and festivals. For a boy, the most important day of his young life comes on a Sabbath near his 13th birthday. Then, after due study and preparation, he becomes Bar Mitzvah (a "son of the commandment"), a full member of the congregation, with a man's religious duties.

Hebrew is taught to all children who attend the synagogue schools. These children go to class three times a week, and start learning the more familiar words of modern Hebrew. The letters at upper right spell Purim, which is the name of a holiday children love. Here the girls are putting Hebrew letters together into words. Hebrew is read and written from right to left. ▶

ISREAL

A nation reborn in the Promised Land

The scholarly tradition is carried on in Israel by Jewish immigrants from many lands like this man from Hungary, seen here reading the Talmud.

Song of Exile

By the rivers of Babylon, there we sat down, yea, we wept, when we remembered Zion.

We hanged our harps upon the willows in the midst thereof.

For there they that carried us away captive required of us a song; . . .

How shall we sing the Lord's song in a strange land?

Psalm 137

"If I forget thee, O Jerusalem, let my right hand forget its cunning," sang Jewish captives in Babylonian exile. Then and since, the Jews never forgot. So the founding of the new state of Israel in 1948 is an historic adventure. It has drawn together Jews from some 65 nations, from North African huts, Nazi death camps, as well as many other backgrounds as different as any to be found on earth.

The Return to Zion, of which Jews have dreamed ever since they were scattered after the fall of Jerusalem in 70 A.D., was the basis of the Zionist movement. In turn Zionism led to the nation of Israel. Many problems and bitter difficulties have arisen, both inside Israel and with surrounding Arab nations. But the Jews in Israel are striving hard to build a new home for Judaism on the rock of the Torah.

Festive Sabbath gets an early start on a religious collective farm in Israel. Here a family is starting on Friday afternoon for the dining hall.

THE FAITH
OF CHRISTIANITY

THE FAITH
OF CHRISTIANITY

OUR FATHER, begins the prayer which Jesus taught his followers in the Sermon on the Mount (*see page 163*). No other religion, not even Judaism, has ever placed such emphasis on the fatherhood of God, or on the fact that *every* human being is more than God's servant —he is God's own child.

The spiritual force of this wonderful teaching has gone far toward making Christianity the most active of all faiths on earth, and the Lord's Prayer by far the most widely used prayer in the history of man. For Christianity is much the largest of all religions. About 850 million people, one out of every three now on earth, are Christians, and they are spread far more widely around the world than the followers of any other faith.

Christianity welcomes all who will acknowledge Christ and try to follow His example. The central points of the Christian faith are in the Apostles' Creed, shown on this page. It is used by Roman Catholics, Anglicans, Presbyterians, Lutherans, Methodists and many others with only a few minor differences in wording. The Eastern Orthodox Church uses a similar but longer wording. Only about five percent of the world's Christians, the largest such groups being the Baptists and Congregationalists, accept no binding creed.

Christianity is based on actual events. Christ's death provides its chief symbol, the Cross (the crucifix on page 119 is a fine 11th Century bronze that is now in Germany). Christianity also places far more emphasis than any of the other great faiths on having its Lord ever

personally present in the *here* and *now*. "Faith in Jesus Christ," writes the great Swiss thinker Emil Brunner, "is participation in an event: in something which has happened, which is happening, and which is going to happen."

Brahman, the supreme Hindu god, is both a personal and an impersonal force. Buddhists believe that their founder Buddha passed into Nirvana nearly 2,500 years ago. Neither Confucianism nor Taoism preaches a personal God. Jews consider their Messiah has not yet come. Mohammed insisted he was only a prophet, and he died in 632 A.D. But Christians believe their Lord rose from the dead to redeem them, and that He lives—now and forever—to help them.

Because it is the most active of all faiths, Christianity is deeply involved in the world around it. This has its risks, but Christians must take them or their religion may lose its living force.

BELIEVE IN GOD THE FATHER ALMIGHTY Maker of heaven and earth:

And in Jesus Christ His only Son our Lord: Who was conceived by the Holy Ghost, born of the Virgin Mary: suffered under Pontius Pilate, was crucified, dead, and buried: He descended into hell: the third day He rose again from the dead: He ascended into heaven, and sitteth on the right hand of God the Father Almighty: from thence He shall come to judge the quick and the dead.

BELIEVE in the Holy Ghost: the holy catholic Church: the communion of saints: the forgiveness of sins: the resurrection of the body: and the life everlasting. *Amen*

In solemn procession behind cross and candles the choir of the Episcopalian National Cathedral in Washington, D.C., marches from the great altar. Christians have long found in music a path to the heart of their faith.

THE LIFE OF CHRIST

Ever since its birth almost 2,000 years ago, Christianity has based itself on two forceful beliefs: that Jesus Christ is the Son of God, and that God sent Christ to earth to live as humans live, suffer as humans suffer, die to redeem mankind and gloriously rise again.

"For God so loved the world, that he gave his only begotten Son, that whosoever believeth in him should not perish, but have everlasting life" (John 3:16). And Paul promises in Romans 5:19, "For as by one man's disobedience many were made sinners, so by the obedience of one shall many be made righteous."

These two ideas separate Christianity from all other religions. To Christians Jesus is not just the founder of Christianity, but the heart of it. Adam and Eve, by disobeying God, sinned. In His wrath, God expelled them from Paradise and thus they and all the humanity descended from them came to know death, which is the result of sin. At the same time God punished Adam and Eve, He foretold the coming of a Redeemer. This Redeemer was Jesus. He was, as the Son of God, divine. But He was also truly human.

The story and spirit of Jesus have inspired some of man's greatest creations. The masterpieces on the following pages cast light upon the earthly life of Jesus Christ. He was born poor. He toiled. He was tempted by the devil. He knew hunger. He thirsted. He suffered on the Cross. He died in agony.

Not until His Resurrection did Christ's life reveal its true purpose. Then His words, "because I live, ye shall live also," took on their full meaning and lifted men to unexpected heights.

THE ADORATION OF THE HOLY CHILD BY THE SHEPHERDS IN THE STABLE The Infant Christ was born in a stable in Bethlehem because Mary and Joseph could find no other place to stay. The Flemish artist Hugo van der Goes, who in 1475 painted this scene of the first Christmas, placed it in his own time and country. ▶

THE TEMPTATION IN THE WILDERNESS *Satan tempts Jesus to turn stones into bread in this painting by Tintoretto of Venice done around 1575. Christ replied, "Man shall not live by bread alone."*

THE BAPTISM IN THE JORDAN *At the start of His active ministry, Christ had John the Baptist perform for Him the ritual of baptism. In a painting (right) by the 15th Century Italian Piero della Francesca, John is shown completing the ceremony as the Holy Spirit descends "like a dove."*

JESUS THE DIVINE TEACHER is shown in this 13th Century French sculpture at Chartres Cathedral. As Christ began to teach of a kingdom "not of this world" and of God as Father, "there followed him great multitudes of people."

CALLING HIS DISCI-
PLES *From the start.*
Jesus moved among hum-
ble folk, gathering a band
to follow Him and spread
his teachings. First to be
chosen were the fishermen
Peter and Andrew on the
Sea of Galilee, shown here
in a painting by Duccio of
Siena around 1308.

THE TRIBUTE MONEY
Around 1427 the Florentine
painter Masaccio showed
St. Peter, at right, paying a
coin to Caesar's tax collec-
tor while Jesus, in center at
left, says to his disciples:
"Render unto Caesar the
things which are Caesar's:
unto God the things which
are God's." ▶

THE STORM ON GALI-LEE *Christ tried to give His disciples a deep faith, but during a tempest on the Sea of Galilee they were overcome by fear. Jesus was asleep in the boat; when they awakened Him, the Bible relates, "He arose and rebuked the wind, and said unto the sea, Peace, be still. And the wind ceased, and there was great calm." Then Jesus asked the disciples, "How is it that ye have no faith?" Delacroix of France painted this around 1853.*

PERFORMING A MIRACLE Christ was often asked to heal the sick and the blind. He emphasized that faith played an important part in the miracles: when a woman who had been in pain for a dozen years was cured by touching His garment, He said: "Daughter . . . thy faith hath made thee whole." This small ivory relief was possibly carved .in Constantinople in the 5th Century.

◀ THE TRANSFIGURATION A key point in Christ's life came with His Transfiguration on a high mountain. Painting about 1480, the Venetian Bellini caught the spell of the moment in which the divinity of Christ was revealed to Peter, James and John.

THE LAST SUPPER: CHRIST FORETELLS HIS BETRAYAL   *The evening before His Crucifixion Jesus shared His final meal with His disciples in the upper room of a house in Jerusalem. Troubled in spirit, He told them: "One of you shall betray me." He asked them to remember His coming sacrifice through the act of eating the bread which "is my body" and drinking the wine which "is my blood."*

In Venice around 1593 Tintoretto re-created the scene, showing eleven of the Twelve Apostles on one side of the table, with the betrayer Judas Iscariot sitting alone, facing Jesus as He offers the bread to a disciple. In the painting, a luminous tumult of angels swirls down into the room, unnoticed either by the apostles intent upon Jesus or by the servants who are hurrying about their duties with the meal.

THE CROWN OF THORNS *After Jesus had been sentenced by Pontius Pilate to be crucified, the Roman soldiery beat Him, mocked Him as the "King of the Jews" and crowned Him with a wreath of thorns. In the agonized image (left) by the French modern, Rouault, the face of Christ holds the suffering of all victims of human cruelty everywhere.*

THE CRUCIFIXION *On Calvary, Christ was nailed to the Cross. Such a death was then degrading; the skulls scattered about were those of common criminals. But the Cross soon became the symbol of Christianity, and the Crucifixion, pictured in this 1477 painting by the Sicilian Antonello da Messina, assumed the beauty of eternal sacrifice it has had ever since.* ▶

THE AGONY IN GETHSEMANE *Praying in the Garden of Gethsemane during the night before His betrayal, Jesus revealed His human dread of the Crucifixion. But as the German Wolf Huber shows in his 1530 painting, Christ's spiritual strength upheld Him, in contrast to the sad fleshly weakness of the disciples, who sleep (left) as the soldiers approach (right) to take Him away.*

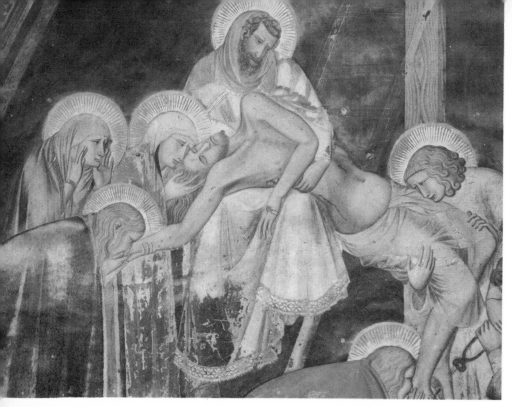

THE DESCENT FROM THE CROSS After the Crucifixion, some of Christ's followers came to take His body to a tomb. The Italian Pietro Lorenzetti painted this fresco about 1325. As the disciples tenderly lift the body of Jesus from the Cross, it assumes an angular line which heightens the scene's mood of anguish.

THE RESURRECTION   Three days after His death, Christ arose triumphant from the tomb. About 1463 the Italian painter Piero della Francesca pictured Him towering over the useless guards set to watch His grave. The painting shows with stark majesty the wonder of His Resurrection and the hope it holds for all men of victory over death. For as Saint Paul wrote to the Corinthians: "If Christ be not risen, then is our preaching vain, and your faith is also vain." ▶

THE ENTOMBMENT The Gospels say that "a rich man of Arimathea, named Joseph . . . went unto Pilate, and begged the body of Jesus." Joseph bought fine linen, wrapped Jesus in it, "and laid Him in a sepulchre . . . hewn out of a rock, and rolled a stone unto the door of the sepulchre." In this 1559 work by Titian, the women are Mary and Mary Magdalene.

CHRIST RISEN

To a vast host of Christians, Jesus Christ is not only risen, showing Himself as in the painting reproduced below, but is actually present in the world today as Christus Pantocrator, the Savior, Teacher, Supreme Judge and All-Ruler (*shown in the mosaic at the right*) Who proclaims, "I am the light of the world."

Beliefs differ in some details, but the Roman Catholic, Orthodox and Anglican churches, along with most Protestant groups, hold that Christ is inseparable from the triune God—the Father, the Son and the Holy Spirit—and that God, in His unity and His trinity, is and always has been present and active in the world. God makes Himself felt in the lives of human beings through the influence of the Third Person of the Trinity, the Holy Spirit.

What Christ said and did on earth has been and is a hope and a guide for millions of men. In the short period of His active ministry, which may have lasted no more than three years, Christ revealed Himself as a man of simple speech but profound wisdom, as a storyteller who could enthrall multitudes and as a being of infinite compassion and love.

All the teachings of Jesus' followers are authorized by the resurrected Christ's final words to His disciples, uttered just before He ascended into heaven: "All power is given unto me in heaven and in earth. Go ye therefore, and teach all nations, baptizing them in the name of the Father, and of the Son and of the Holy Ghost; teaching them to observe all things whatsoever I have commanded you: and, lo, I am with you alway, even unto the end of the world."

CHRISTUS PANTOCRATOR. In this enormous mosaic above the altar of the cathedral at Monreale in Sicily, Christ as Pantocrator (the Greek for "All-Ruler") holds His right hand in the gesture of blessing. Directly below Him is the Virgin Mary holding the infant Jesus on her lap. On either side of her are angels and saints. ▶

THE SUPPER AT EMMAUS After His Resurrection Christ revealed Himself often, but never more movingly than at Emmaus when He "sat at meat" with two of his disciples, and "took bread, and blessed it, and brake, and gave to them. And their eyes were opened, and they knew him." Rembrandt painted this version of the scene in 1648.

Sea of Galilee, where Jesus calmed the waves and walked on the water, is 13 miles long. Near it are Nazareth, where Jesus grew up; Cana, where He turned water to wine in his first miracle; and Capernaum, where He often preached.

Valley of Elah (below, in background) is the scene of David's encounter with Goliath around 1000 B.C. The Philistines, after whom Palestine is named, used the valley to go inland from the coastal plain below Joppa. Bethlehem (picture at right) is to the East.

PALESTINE, THE COUNTRY OF GOD

The spiritual impact of the Holy Land or Palestine has powerfully influenced Western civilization. Its classic boundaries (*see map, pages 142–43*) are from Dan to Beer-sheba (150 miles) and from Gaza to the Dead Sea (54 miles). This is barely 6,000 square miles. Even including the territory east of the River Jordan, the Holy Land is smaller in area than Maryland or Albania. The borders of the modern state of Israel are roughly similar.

It is a land hemmed in on the south and east by wilderness and desert. To the north rise steep mountains. To the west is the Mediterranean, breaking against a coast that offers little shelter to ships. Never the seat of great material cultures such as those of neighboring Egypt and Babylonia, Palestine has yet been a focal point of history for 4,000 years. The great trade routes of the Ancient World traversed it, and through them the world first learned of Palestine's unique possession, the Judaeo-Christian heritage which has since strongly shaped events in the Western world. Naaman the Leper, "captain of the host of the

King of Syria," summed up that heritage after Elisha had cured him: "Behold, now I know that there is no God in all the earth, but in Israel."

The holy city of the Holy Land is Jerusalem (*below, with map at right*). An Egyptian outpost before King David took it about 1000 B.C., Jerusalem was a spot that promised obscurity: it lacked a harbor and dominated no main roads. But the hill-fort was near Beer-sheba, Hebron, Bethlehem, Bethel and Shiloh, where altars had been raised to God; its central location made it a convenient political capital; and the Temple that Solomon built provided a platform for prophets. In Old Testament times its streets were swept, its markets inspected. When the sunrise lit its enfolding mists, it looked indeed "the city which the Lord did choose out of all the tribes of Israel, to put his name there" (I Kings 14:21). But

The City of Jerusalem is shown below in a picture made near the Mount of Olives. The blue Moslem Dome of the Rock appears at right center.

4,000-year-old Jerusalem (its name means "City of Peace") has seen little peace. For Jews and Christians the most sacred of places, for Moslems surpassed only by Mecca and Madinat an-Nabi (Medina), it remains divided by war.

The River Jordan, in which Jesus was baptized, flows east of Jerusalem. It is rarely more than 10 feet in depth or 100 feet in width, but its water is vital to the Holy Land.

Many of the sites named in the Bible can

Sacred places in Jerusalem are on the map right, *located according to best evidence.* ▶

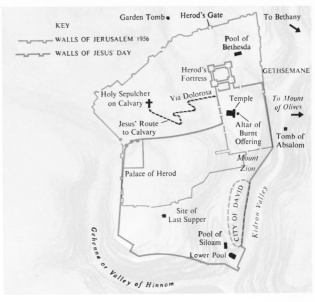

River Jordan rises in north of Holy Land and enters Dead Sea at 1,292 feet below sea level. Its name means "descender."

BIBLE LAND

ITS SOIL HAS FELT WEIGHT OF GREAT EVENTS

As Biblical times have gone farther into the past, modern man has learned more and more about them. Since 1920 archaeologists have made more progress than ever before in the Holy Land, and discovery of the Dead Sea Scrolls has speeded the pace.

Although the details shown on this map, including costumes and architecture, are based on the best research, much remains unknown. The locations of Sodom, Gomorrah and Tirzah, one of Israel's ancient capitals, can be only approximated. The first two probably stood in the area now covered by the Dead Sea, which has grown since Lot fled. The exact sites of Job's lamentations, of Abraham's sacrifice, and Christ's baptism may always be debated. Most other scenes and place names on the map are discussed on nearby pages or elsewhere in the book. Arrows indicate locations off the map.

be identified. After he had married Rebekah, Isaac dug three wells at Beer-sheba and today Arab girls still draw water there in dress that has changed little from Rebekah's time. The wilderness into which Isaac's half-brother Ishmael was cast with his mother Hagar is still desolate today, as it was when Moses led his

people through it during 40 years of wandering.

Among the other places shown on the map (*above*) are Jericho, where Moses' successor Joshua won a great victory in his conquest of the land of Canaan, and Shiloh, where Samuel heard the voice of God. Solomon built the Temple in Jerusalem with "timber of cedar

and . . . timber of fir" which King Hiram of Tyre harvested in Lebanon and shipped by sea to Joppa. Among the prophets who worshiped in the Temple was Isaiah who, for forty years and under four kings of David's line, served his people as a statesman, teacher and spokesman for righteousness. Farther north, near Tirzah, Gideon (one of the early Judges) chose 300 from his army of 32,000, and then triumphed over the Midianites. Next to Jericho lies Gilgal, where Samuel and the Israelites hailed Saul as king to lead them. After Samuel died Saul enlisted the Witch of En-dor to raise up Samuel to counsel him.

143

THE ONWARD MARCH
OF CHRISTIAN FAITH

Among all the religions by which men seek to worship, Christianity is the most widely spread, has the most followers and makes the greatest claims for the divinity of its Founder and the finality of its teaching.

In the 2,000 years since Jesus lived on earth, the churches in which Christians worship have developed such an amazing variety of belief and practice that it is sometimes hard to recognize that they all acknowledge the same Lord. The glittering spectacle of an Easter Mass in St. Peter's, Rome; the quiet service within the bare walls of a Quaker meetinghouse; the squatting circle of Congo tribesmen around the white-haired medical missionary; the Orthodox monks cut off from the world on the forbidden peak of Mount Athos—how can these and hundreds of other different examples, all be accounted parts of the same whole that is named Christianity?

But all, under whatever form, acknowledge one God; all declare their loyalty to one Lord; all find in one Cross the symbol of their faith. The differences are many and confusing, and often weaken Christianity. It is not true, as one of the hymns most sung by Christians puts it: "We are not divided/ All one body we/ One in hope and doctrine/ One in charity." But in their final allegiance, they are one. They are Christians.

The inevitable questions rise: Where did this Christian religion come from? How did it spread? Why has it taken so many forms? The answers make up one of the most dramatic and, in some parts, romantic stories known to history. The following short account can tell only some of the highlights of that long record.

Christianity is the religion which springs historically from Jesus of Nazareth. He told the Apostles He chose: "Even as my Father hath sent me, even so send I you" (John 20:21). The Apostles chose others to ordain, and this living chain from one human generation to the next continues today (*picture at left*).

Ordination, when a bishop places his hands on the head of a candidate and bestows on him the power of a minister, carries on the process begun by Jesus when he chose his Apostles.

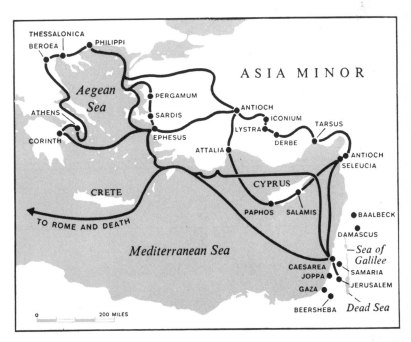

St. Paul's travels to spread the Gospel took him through Asia Minor and the Mediterranean area. He sought out cities where no Christian had ever preached before.

At traditional site of Christ's tomb, members of the Coptic Church (right) *hold Holy Saturday rites.* ▶

The two great early leaders were St. Peter and St. Paul. The Gospels record that Peter was the first openly to salute Jesus as the Messiah. Jesus said, "Thou art Peter, and upon this rock I will build my church, . . . And I will give unto thee the keys of the kingdom of heaven." And when, 50 days after Christ's Resurrection, His followers made their first attempt to win a public hearing, it was Peter who preached the sermon. Later he preached and taught in many places, finally reaching Rome where he is believed to have suffered martyrdom under the Roman Emperor, Nero, about 65 A.D.

Paul was a Jew born in Tarsus, a city now in south Turkey. In his early years he actively fought Christianity. In 35 A.D., as he was rid-

At manger in Bethlehem, believed to be site of Christ's birth, two monks kneel in prayer before a tiny statue of the Infant Jesus.

On Way of the Cross in Jerusalem on Good Friday, pilgrims carry a huge cross step by step along Christ's route.

ing to Damascus to destroy a company of Christians there, he had a vision of Jesus and became the greatest Christian missionary of all times. After preaching his way possibly as far west as Spain, tradition says he was finally beheaded in Rome about 65 A.D.

In Peter and Paul the Christian religion can be seen beginning to develop along both its great avenues. It develops as an institution (the Church) and as a teaching, a theology, a faith. The institution is named first because the theology came out of it, not the institution out of the

At 12th Station on Way of the Cross, Roman Catholic priests hold Good Friday services at a Greek Orthodox altar.

theology. The New Testament—Gospels, Epistles, Apocalypse—is a product of the church. Little of the New Testament was written until there was a flourishing church all over the Roman world. The New Testament was not gathered in its finally agreed-on form until 692.

For 250 years after the martyrdoms of Peter and Paul the Christian church continued to spread steadily over the Mediterranean. In 284, the Roman Emperor Diocletian began the worst of all persecutions of Christians. By 305 Diocletian gave up his effort to destroy the

Sturdy tower and east end of Anglican cathedral (right) at Wells in England are mirrored in a flower-lined pond.

young religion. A war between rivals for Emperor followed which was won by Constantine. It is said that Constantine, before the decisive battle, saw a vision of a lighted Cross in the afternoon sky and the words *"In hoc signo vinces"* ("In this sign conquer"). Soon Christianity became the official religion of the Roman Empire.

In this same period many men tried to protect the spiritual message of Christianity by withdrawing from worldly contacts. The deserts and lonely places around the Mediterranean received many solitary hermits. This movement developed into the establishment of monasteries and convents for monks and nuns. A notable champion of early monasticism was St. Jerome, the scholar who translated into Latin both Old and New Testaments from their Hebrew and Greek originals. His version, the Vulgate, is the Bible of the Roman Catholic Church of this day. Another great early monk was St. Benedict, who founded the Benedictines.

Church inside Kremlin in Moscow is the Cathedral of the Annunciation. Now a museum, it is a favorite for sightseers. It was long a favored church of the czars and their families.

One of the greatest of all splits among Christians began after Constantine moved to his new capital of Constantinople (now Istanbul). The Eastern Orthodox churches, which now have 150 million followers, began in the Holy Land before there were any Christians in Rome. Like Roman Catholicism, Orthodoxy (from the Greek *orthos,* "true" or "upright," and *doxa,* "belief") considers that it was founded directly by Jesus. For Christianity's first thousand years the two together comprised the One, Holy, Catholic and Apostolic Church. But cracks in the unity appeared early. The two great centers—Rome headed by its Pope and Constantinople headed by its Patriarch—were competing for converts and power. In 1054 a tragic break came. Today Orthodoxy considers Rome

heretical, and Rome in turn considers that Orthodoxy is schismatic.

Meanwhile the Christian Church was steadily widening its boundaries to the far corners of Europe and into Asia and Africa. It suffered severe setbacks after the swift rise of Islam in the 7th Century. An Islamic army reached central France before being driven back in 732 by Charles Martel. The Turks besieged Vienna as late as 1683, holding Greece and much of the Balkans into the 19th Century, casting a cloud over the Eastern Orthodox churches there and elsewhere that still exists.

The medieval period, especially as it flow-

Consecrating a U. S. Bishop (right), *a Russian Orthodox prelate holds up candelabra as he blesses the people.* ▶

150

ered in the early 13th Century, has been held by many to be the peak of the Church's glory. It was "the age of faith," an age when the authority of the Church was accepted almost without question. Marvelous monuments to the religious devotion of that time are in the cathedrals. Their glory has for generations drawn pilgrims from all over the globe. Today the worshiper within their walls still finds in the lofty vaults and inspired ornaments a lasting expression of the Christian faith that created them.

In Rome, where St. Peter's is the largest of all cathedrals, the present Pope, Pius XII, has authority over both Vatican City, the world's smallest temporal state, and the Roman Catholic Church, which is Christendom's largest,

In St. Peter's Basilica Pope Pius XII officiates from his throne at a ceremony when new cardinals are made. ▶

most powerful spiritual domain. Vatican City itself covers only 108.7 acres, but the Pope wields spiritual power—through 62 cardinals, 1,427 bishops, some 700,000 priests and 970,000 nuns—over some 484 million souls served by 410,000 Catholic churches all around the world.

At the Renaissance height of its ecclesiastical pomp and power, Roman Catholicism was challenged by a widespread, urgent call for a return to early Christian simplicity. The Protestant Reformation, which resulted, now has more than 200 million followers—one-fourth of the world's Christians. It was led by bold but devout men ready to die for their beliefs.

State of Vatican City dominates foreground of this picture, with domed St. Peter's in center.

The first rumblings against Roman Catholicism came in movements by the Waldensians, Wycliffites and Hussites. The Waldensians, who believe any Christian can be his own priest, still live in the Alpine valleys where they retreated after Peter Waldo's excommunication in 1184. The Englishman John Wycliffe, preaching in a quiet country church and at Oxford, attacked such Catholic practices as pilgrimages and the sale of indulgences. Wycliffe inspired John Hus, in distant Bohemia, and after Hus was martyred in 1415 his followers founded the Moravian Church.

The full-scale Reformation began in 1517, when the German monk Martin Luther attacked papal authority. Luther felt that the essence of Christianity lay not in an elaborate organization headed by the Pope, but in each believer's humble, direct communion with God, seeking "that righteousness by which through grace and sheer mercy God justifies us through faith." The Lutherans now number some 70 million followers in the world.

The other "father of the Reformation" was John Calvin, a Frenchman who was forced to flee from France because of his views and settled at Geneva in Switzerland. His *Institutes of the Christian Religion* remains the greatest of all Protestant theological works. The Presbyterian and Reformed churches, the spiritual heirs of Calvinism, now have some 41 million members.

The Church of England broke with the Papacy under King Henry VIII, declaring: "The Bishop of Rome hath not by Scripture any greater authority in England than any other foreign bishop." Its doctrines have remained Catholic as well as Protestant. The world-wide Anglican Church, which includes Episcopalians in the United States, now has about 40 million members.

Because Anglicanism did not have the plainness that so many Protestants desired, the Reformation raged on in England after settling down elsewhere. One of its notable figures was John Bunyan, a forerunner of the present Baptists, who now have 22 million members. An Anglican in youth, Bunyan later wrote *Pilgrim's Progress*, one of the great works of the Reformation. He defied authority and went to prison repeatedly for his beliefs. The same was true of George Fox, whose vision from Pendle Hill

Waldensian women in ancestral dress sing psalms after church in an Italian Alpine valley. The Waldensians have long been Protestants, starting with Peter Waldo in the 12th Century.

Wycliffe's Church near Oxford in England was the scene of John Wycliffe's influential preaching from 1368 to 1374. While here, Wycliffe first became deeply aware of how much religion could mean to ordinary people.

Quaker's vision came to George Fox as he saw view (above) from Pendle Hill in England and was "moved to sound the day of the Lord."

Pilgrim's Port in Delfshaven, Holland, is marked by a church where the Pilgrims worshiped before leaving for America.

in 1652 led him to found the Society of Friends, also known as Quakers because a hostile judge thought Fox quaked before the Lord.

In New England, the Quakers were harassed by the Separatists, who had only recently escaped from Anglican tyranny and are ancestors of today's Congregationalists, Unitarians and Universalists. The original Pilgrim Fathers had banded together in England and emigrated to Holland in 1608. They sailed for America in 1620.

The inspiration for the last large church that came out of the Reformation was from an Anglican clergyman, John Wesley, who never intended a break at all. Wesley made a preaching

Methodism's shrine is chapel (right) which John Wesley built in 1777 in London. He often preached there.

Martin Luther, leader of the Reformation

John Calvin, a great Reformation figure

campaign throughout England for more than 50 years. But he remained an Anglican until he died in 1791. However, his followers began a church, called Methodist for its methodical organization, that stressed the personal approach to religion. "A Methodist," wrote Wesley, "is one who has the love of God shed abroad in his heart by the Holy Ghost given unto him. . . . God is the joy of his heart and

St. Ignatius Loyala, founder of Jesuits

the desire of his soul, which is constantly crying out, '. . My God and my all! Thou art the strength of my heart, and my portion forever!' " Simple fervor—like that of Luther, Calvin and Protestantism's other leaders—brought a quickening of faith which has been the Reformation's most lasting result.

Shocked by the revolt of Luther and Calvin, the Roman Catholic Church began its own period of internal reform and external attack on the Protestant advance that is usually called the Counter Reformation. The Council of Trent ended many abuses and laid down a body of Catholic doctrine that is still definitive. A main accomplishment of the Counter Reformation was the organization and spread of the Society of Jesus—the Jesuit order which stopped Protestantism in its tracks in Hungary and Poland, won back to papal allegiance much of Germany and most of France, spread excellent schools over Europe and thrust Catholic missions into India, Japan, China and the New World.

Ulm Cathedral, floodlit in green, thrusts its tower 528 feet into the night sky, far above old German city. Begun under the Papacy, it was completed by Lutherans. ▶

Massacre of St. Bartholomew (above) *began in Paris in 1572 with murder of leading French Prot-*
estants by the Catholics, who included the troops of the Duke of Guise.

Ignatius Loyola, the founder of the Society of Jesus, is a figure as fascinating as any of the Protestant reformers. A Spanish grandee whose military career had been ended by wounds, he became a student at the University of Paris, where he gathered half a dozen devoted companions—one of them Francis Xavier, later to become the missionary saint to India and the East. In 1534 this little group—later formally named the Society of Jesus—took an oath St. Ignatius proposed. As a former soldier who had

dedicated his armor to the Virgin Mary, he established a military company with discipline as strict as in any army. His *Spiritual Exercises* remain the world's most famous manual of discipline for the individual will.

The Wars of Religion between Protestants and Catholics in the century from 1550 to 1650 brought the Reformation to a bloody climax. On both sides the record is stained with ferocity. In France the Protestant Huguenots opposed the Catholics and the atrocities culminated in the six-week-long Massacre of St. Bartholomew from which French Protestantism never fully recovered. In England the Catholic queen Mary Tudor ("Bloody Mary") martyred many Protestants, and the Protestant queen Elizabeth executed the Catholics she found plotting to dethrone her. When Catholic Ireland rose up against Oliver Cromwell, he crushed the revolt in a way the Irish have never forgotten or forgiven. There was also much religious violence in Belgium, Holland, Germany, Spain and elsewhere; the Spanish Inquisition has ever since remained a symbol of bigotry and persecution.

Even during the Wars of Religion there began a far happier Christian development: the great missionary surge which has planted churches in all parts of the world.

Christ's birth, which happened so modestly so long ago, marked the greatest watershed in history. The religion which was born out of that event developed mankind's most enduring and widespread institution, the Christian Church. The Church has taken many forms. Its divisions are old and distressing. But the Christian Church as a whole is even greater than the sum of its parts. More people are now trying to lead Christian lives than at any time since the Resurrection. And today Christianity in the West is well into the most productive intellectual period it has known since the 16th Century.

What, then, is the outlook for Christianity and its churches? It is not one to justify easy optimism, but it is far from hopeless. There is a wide sense of unsatisfied spiritual needs among men, and also a wide sense of how inadequate are other answers to their problems. This is a time of opportunity for Christianity.

Thoughtful Christians see the weaknesses of the churches. If Christianity is responsible for the character of human civilization, then its task is hardly more than begun. But never has the figure of Christ risen higher or in more compelling majesty over the debris of human failure. Never has the Cross stood out more clearly as the symbol of man's ultimate hope.

Christians fight Moslems near Granada at the Battle of La Higuera in Spain in 1431. The Moslems managed to save Granada and hold it until the year 1492.

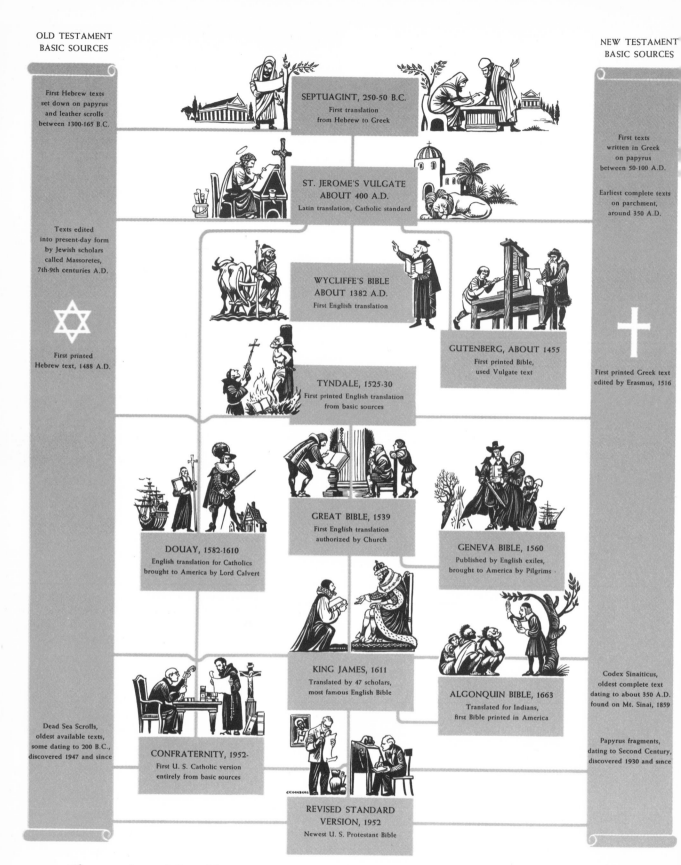

First Hebrew texts
set down on papyrus
and leather scrolls
between 1300-165 B.C.

First texts
written in Greek
on papyrus
between 50-100 A.D.

Earliest complete texts
on parchment,
around 350 A.D.

Texts edited
into present-day form
by Jewish scholars
called Massoretes,
7th-9th centuries A.D.

First printed
Hebrew text, 1488 A.D.

First printed Greek text
edited by Erasmus, 1516

Dead Sea Scrolls,
oldest available texts,
some dating to 200 B.C.,
discovered 1947 and since

Codex Sinaiticus,
oldest complete text
dating to about 350 A.D.
found on Mt. Sinai, 1859

Papyrus fragments,
dating to Second Century,
discovered 1930 and since

SEPTUAGINT, 250-50 B.C.
First translation
from Hebrew to Greek

ST. JEROME'S VULGATE
ABOUT 400 A.D.
Latin translation, Catholic standard

WYCLIFFE'S BIBLE
ABOUT 1382 A.D.
First English translation

GUTENBERG, ABOUT 1455
First printed Bible,
used Vulgate text

TYNDALE, 1525-30
First printed English translation
from basic sources

GREAT BIBLE, 1539
First English translation
authorized by Church

DOUAY, 1582-1610
English translation for Catholics
brought to America by Lord Calvert

GENEVA BIBLE, 1560
Published by English exiles,
brought to America by Pilgrims

KING JAMES, 1611
Translated by 47 scholars,
most famous English Bible

ALGONQUIN BIBLE, 1663
Translated for Indians,
first Bible printed in America

CONFRATERNITY, 1952-
First U. S. Catholic version
entirely from basic sources

REVISED STANDARD
VERSION, 1952
Newest U. S. Protestant Bible

The genealogy of the Bible, from the earliest Hebrew to the latest American versions, is given in the chart above which illustrates the most famous Greek, Latin and English translations. The long panels at the sides list some of the basic texts available, and the lines show what was drawn upon by each translation. Some of the Bible's translators have suffered, or even died, for their devotion.

THE BIBLE, MOST SACRED OF BOOKS

The New Testament has shaped Western civilization more decisively than anything else ever written. Largely gathered between the years 50 and 100 A.D., it tells the beginnings of Christianity. The four Gospels tell of the birth, teaching, death and Resurrection of Jesus Christ. Then come: the Acts of the Apostles, a history of the early Christian movement; the Epistles, or letters to the church groups that soon spread around the Mediterranean; and the Book of Revelation, a visionary account of the final triumph of God's purpose.

The new religion that was to affect mankind so deeply was first preached in Jerusalem just after Christ's Ascension. It grew so fast that a thriving church existed even before the first parts of the New Testament, probably some of Paul's Epistles, were put down to help his congregations. Soon the Gospels and the Acts were written, though centuries passed before the entire New Testament was assembled in its finally agreed-on form. Not until the year 1560 was an English translation divided into separate verses.

The selections below, all from the famous King James version, are printed in paragraphs for easier reading. Where more than one book or chapter is quoted, the combined sources are listed at the end of the passage.

The most famous of all Christ's teachings is the Sermon on the Mount, which fills three whole chapters of Matthew. Among many other noble passages, it includes the Beatitudes ("Blessed are . . .") and the Lord's Prayer. Some authorities think it is too long to have been a single sermon, and is rather a collection of Jesus' sayings at various times. In any case, it is a wonderful example of the message of Jesus as Teacher and Savior.

Oldest Bible text thus far discovered is the fragment above from a Dead Sea scroll showing part of the first book of Samuel 23:9–16.

THE SERMON ON THE MOUNT

And seeing the multitudes, he went up into a mountain: and when he was set, his disciples came unto him: and he opened his mouth, and taught them, saying,

Blessed are the poor in spirit: for theirs is the kingdom of heaven. Blessed are they that mourn: for they shall be comforted. Blessed are the meek: for they shall inherit the earth. Blessed are they which do hunger and thirst after righteousness: for they shall be filled. Blessed are the merciful: for they shall obtain mercy. Blessed are the pure in heart: for they shall see God. Blessed are the peacemakers: for they shall be called the children of God. Blessed are they which are persecuted for righteousness' sake: for theirs is the kingdom of heaven. Blessed are ye, when men shall revile you, and persecute you, and shall say all manner of evil against you falsely, for my sake. Rejoice; and be exceeding glad: for great is your reward in heaven: for so persecuted they the prophets which were before you. . . .

Ye are the salt of the earth: but if the salt have lost his savor, wherewith shall it be salted? it is thenceforth good for nothing, but to be cast out, and to be trodden under foot of men. Ye are the light of the world. . . . Let your light so shine before men, that they may see your good works, and glorify your Father which is in heaven....

Ye have heard that it hath been said, An eye for an eye, and a tooth for a tooth: but I say unto you, That ye resist not evil: but whosoever shall smite thee on thy right cheek, turn to him the other also. And if any man will sue thee at the law, and take away thy coat, let him have thy cloak also. And whosoever shall compel thee to go a mile, go with him twain. Give to him that asketh thee, and from him that would borrow of thee turn not thou away.

Ye have heard that it hath been said, Thou shalt love thy neighbor, and hate thine enemy. But I say unto you, Love your enemies, bless them that curse you, do good to them that hate you, and pray for them which despitefully use you, and persecute you; that ye may be the children of your Father which is in heaven: for he maketh his sun to rise on the evil and on the good, and sendeth rain on the just and on the unjust. For if ye love them which love you, what reward have ye? do not even the publicans the same? And if ye salute your brethren only ... do not even the publicans so? Be ye therefore perfect, even as your Father which is in heaven is perfect.

Take heed that ye do not your alms before men to be seen of them: otherwise ye have no reward of your Father which is in heaven. Therefore when thou doest thine alms, do not sound a trumpet before thee.... Let not thy left hand know what thy right hand doeth ... and thy Father which seeth in secret himself shall reward thee openly.

And when thou prayest, thou shalt not be as the hypocrites are: for they love to pray standing in the synagogues and in the corners of the streets, that they may be seen of men.... But thou, when thou prayest, enter into thy closet, and ... pray to thy Father which is in secret; and thy Father which seeth in secret shall reward thee openly....

After this manner therefore pray ye: Our Father which art in heaven, hallowed be thy name. Thy kingdom come. Thy will be done in earth, as it is in heaven. Give us this day our daily bread. And forgive us our debts, as we forgive our debtors. And lead us not into temptation, but deliver us from evil.... Amen.

For if ye forgive men their trespasses, your heavenly Father will also forgive you: but if ye forgive not men their trespasses, neither will your Father forgive your trespasses.... When ye fast, be not, as the hypocrites, of a sad countenance: for they disfigure their faces, that they may appear unto men to fast.... But thou, when thou fastest, anoint thine head, and wash thy face; that thou appear not unto men to fast, but unto thy Father which is in secret: and thy Father ... shall reward thee openly.

Lay not up for yourselves treasures upon earth ... but lay up for yourselves treasures in heaven, where neither moth nor rust doth corrupt, and where thieves do not break through nor steal: for where your treasure is, there will your heart be also.... No man can serve two masters: for either he will hate the one, and love

the other; or else he will hold to the one, and despise the other. Ye cannot serve God and mammon. Therefore I say unto you, Take no thought for your life ... nor yet for your body, what ye shall put on. Is not the life more than meat, and the body than raiment? Behold the fowls of the air: for they sow not, neither do they reap, nor gather into barns; yet your heavenly Father feedeth them. Are ye not much better than they? ...

Consider the lilies of the field, how they grow; they toil not, neither do they spin: and yet I say unto you, That even Solomon in all his glory was not arrayed like one of these. Wherefore, if God so clothe the grass of the field, which today is, and tomorrow is cast into the oven, shall he not much more clothe you, O ye of little faith? ... But seek ye first the kingdom of God ... and all these things shall be added unto you. Take therefore no thought for the morrow: for the morrow shall take thought for the things of itself. Sufficient unto the day is the evil thereof.

Judge not, that ye be not judged. For with what judgment ye judge, ye shall be judged: and with what measure ye mete, it shall be measured to you again. And why beholdest thou the mote that is in thy brother's eye, but considerest not the beam that is in thine own eye? Or how wilt thou say to thy brother, Let me pull out the mote out of thine eye: and, behold, a beam is in thine own eye? Thou hypocrite, first cast out the beam out of thine own eye; and then shalt thou see clearly to cast out the mote out of thy brother's eye. Give not that which is holy unto the dogs, neither cast ye your pearls before swine, lest they trample them under their feet, and turn again and rend you.

Ask, and it shall be given you; seek, and ye shall find; knock, and it shall be opened unto you: for every one that asketh receiveth; and he that seeketh findeth; and to him that knocketh it shall be opened. Or what man is there of you, whom if his son ask bread, will he give him a stone? Or if he ask a fish, will he give him a serpent? ...

Ye shall know them by their fruits. Do men gather grapes of thorns, or figs of thistles? Even so every good tree bringeth forth good fruit; but a corrupt tree bringeth forth evil fruit.... Wherefore by their fruits ye shall know them....

Therefore whosoever heareth these sayings of mine, and doeth them, I will liken him unto a wise man, which built his house upon a rock: and the rain descended, and the floods came, and the winds blew, and beat upon that house; and it fell not: for it was founded upon a rock. And every one that heareth these sayings of mine, and doeth them not, shall be likened unto a foolish man, which built his house upon the sand: and the rain descended, and the floods came, and the winds blew, and beat upon that house; and it fell: and great was the fall of it.

And it came to pass, when Jesus had ended these sayings, the people were astonished at his doctrine: for he taught them as one having authority, and not as the scribes.

—MATTHEW 5–7

The story of St. Paul is partly told in an old illustrated manuscript now in Rome. At top right he is blinded on road to Damascus, and is asked by Jesus, "Why persecutest thou me?" Later he takes name of Paul.

The four Gospel writers appear in a richly orna-mented 8th Century manuscript. At left is St. Luke with an ox.

MIRACLES

Throughout His short period of active ministry on earth, which may have lasted only a year and was certainly no more than four years, Jesus worked an astonishing number of miracles. Some 35 are described in the Gospels, while many more are mentioned without details. He did not perform them to win followers, or to impress important people, but in compassion and in response to simple faith in Him. Even among Christians, attitudes toward His miracles have varied greatly, but these stories have played a large part in the spread of Christianity for nearly two thousand years.

When he had ended all his sayings in the audience of the people, he entered into Capernaum. And a certain centurion's servant, who was dear unto him, was sick, and ready to die. And when he heard of Jesus, he sent unto him the elders of the Jews, beseeching him that he would come and heal his servant. And when they came to Jesus, they besought him instantly, saying, That he was worthy for whom he should do this: for he loved our nation, and he hath built us a synagogue. Then Jesus went with him. And when he was now not far from the house, the centurion sent friends to him, saying . . . Lord, trouble not thyself: for I am not worthy that thou shouldest enter under my roof: wherefore neither thought I myself worthy to come unto thee: but say in a word, and my servant shall be healed. For I also am a man set under authority having under me soldiers, and I say unto one, Go, and he goeth; and to another, Come, and he cometh; and to my servant, Do this, and he doeth. When Jesus heard these things, he marvelled at him, and turned him about, and said unto the people that followed him, I say unto you, I have not found so great faith, no, not in Israel. And they that were sent, returning to the house, found the servant whole that had been sick. . . .

Now when he came nigh to the gate of the city, be-hold, there was a dead man carried out, the only son of his mother, and she was a widow. . . . And when the Lord saw her, he had compassion on her, and said unto her, Weep not. And he came and touched the bier. . . .

Each Gospel maker is shown with his symbol. At left St. Matthew listens attentively to his symbol, the angel.

St. Mark, who wrote what is believed to be the earliest of the four Gospels, is shown turning toward a lion.

And he said, Young man, I say unto thee, Arise. And he that was dead sat up, and began to speak. And he delivered him to his mother. And there came a fear on all: and they glorified God. . . . Then Jesus answering said unto them, Go your way, and tell . . . how that the blind see, the lame walk, the lepers are cleansed, the deaf hear, the dead are raised, to the poor the gospel is preached. . . .

After these things, Jesus went over the sea of Galilee . . . And a great multitude followed him, because they saw his miracles which he did on them that were diseased. And Jesus went up into a mountain. . . . When Jesus then lifted up his eyes, and saw a great company come unto him, he saith unto Philip, Whence shall we buy bread, that these may eat? . . . Philip answered him, Two hundred pennyworth of bread is not sufficient for them, that every one of them may take a little. One of his disciples, Andrew, Simon Peter's brother, saith unto him, There is a lad here, which hath five barley loaves, and two small fishes: but what are they among so many? And Jesus said, Make the men sit down. Now there was much grass in the place. So the men sat down, in number about five thousand.

And Jesus took the loaves; and when he had given thanks, he distributed to the disciples, and the disciples to them that were set down; and likewise of the fishes as much as they would. When they were filled, he said unto his disciples, Gather up the fragments that remain, that nothing be lost. Therefore they gathered them together, and filled twelve baskets with the fragments of the five barley loaves, which remained over and above unto them that had eaten. Then those men, when they had seen the miracle that Jesus did, said, This is of a truth that prophet that should come into the world. . . .

Now a certain man was sick, named Lazarus, of Bethany, the town of Mary and her sister Martha. . . . When Jesus came, he found that he had lain in the grave four days already. . . . Jesus wept. Then said the Jews, Behold how he loved him! And some of them said, Could not this man, which opened the eyes of the blind, have caused that even this man should not have died? . . . And Jesus lifted up his eyes, and . . . cried with a loud voice, Lazarus, come forth. And he that was dead came forth, bound hand and foot with graveclothes. . . . Jesus saith unto them, Loose him, and let him go. Then many of the Jews which came to Mary, and had seen the things which Jesus did, believed on him. . . .

—LUKE 7; JOHN 6, 11.

St. John, who wrote what is believed to be the latest of the four Gospels, is shown at right with an eagle.

167

PARABLES

An old form of teaching is the parable, which has been called "an earthly story with a heavenly meaning." Jesus told more than 40 parables in the course of His ministry, and no one else has ever used this old method of teaching so memorably and effectively.

The same day went Jesus out of the house, and . . . spake many things unto them in parables, saying, Behold, a sower went forth to sow; and when he sowed, some seeds fell by the way side, and the fowls came and devoured them up: some fell upon .stony places, where they had not much earth: and forthwith they sprung up, because they had no deepness of earth: and when the sun was up, they were scorched; and because they had no root, they withered away. And some fell among thorns; and the thorns sprung up, and choked them: but other fell into good ground, and brought forth fruit,

some an hundredfold, some sixtyfold, some thirtyfold. Who hath ears to hear, let him hear. . . .

Another parable put he forth . . . saying, The kingdom of heaven is likened unto a man which sowed good seed in his field: but while men slept, his enemy came and sowed tares among the wheat, and went his way. But when the blade was sprung up, and brought forth fruit, there appeared the tares also. So the servants of the householder came and said unto him, Sir, didst not thou sow good seed in thy field? From whence then hath it tares? He said unto them, An enemy hath done this. The servants said unto him, Wilt thou then that we go and gather them up? But he said, Nay; lest while ye gather up the tares, ye root up also the wheat with them. Let both grow together until the harvest: and in the time of harvest I will say to the reapers, Gather . . . the tares, and . . . burn them: but gather the wheat into my barn. . . .

Then Jesus sent the multitude away . . . and his disciples came unto him, saying, Declare unto us the parable of the tares of the field. He answered and said unto

168

them, He that soweth the good seed is the Son of man: the field is the world: the good seed are the children of the kingdom; but the tares are the children of the wicked one; the enemy that sowed them is the devil; the harvest is the end of the world; and the reapers are the angels. As therefore the tares are gathered and burned in the fire; so shall it be in the end of this world. The Son of man shall send forth his angels, and they shall gather out of his kingdom all things that offend, and them which do iniquity; and shall cast them into a furnace of fire: there shall be wailing and gnashing of teeth. Then shall the righteous shine forth as the sun in the kingdom of their Father. . . .

And, behold, a certain lawyer . . . said unto Jesus, And who is my neighbor? And Jesus answering said, A certain man went down from Jerusalem to Jericho, and fell among thieves, which stripped him of his raiment, and wounded him, and departed, leaving him half dead. And by chance there came down a certain priest that way: and when he saw him, he passed by on the other side. And likewise a Levite . . . passed on the other side. But a certain Samaritan, as he journeyed . . . had compassion on him, and went to him, and bound up his wounds, pouring in oil and wine, and set him on his own beast, and brought him to an inn, and took care of him. And on the morrow when he departed, he took out two pence, and gave them to the host, and said unto him, Take care of him; and whatsoever thou spendest more, when I come again, I will repay thee.

Which now of these three . . . was neighbor unto him that fell among the thieves? And he said, He that showed mercy on him. Then said Jesus unto him, Go, and do thou likewise. . . .

Then drew near unto him all the publicans and sinners for to hear him. And the Pharisees and scribes murmured, saying, This man receiveth sinners, and eateth with them. And he spake this parable unto them, saying, What man of you, having an hundred sheep, if he lose one of them, doth not leave the ninety and nine . . . and go after that which is lost . . . ? And when he hath found it, he layeth it on his shoulders, rejoicing. And when he cometh home, he calleth together his friends and neighbors, saying unto them, Rejoice with me; for I have found my sheep which was lost. I say unto you, that likewise joy shall be in heaven over one sinner, that repenteth, more than over ninety and nine just persons, which need no repentance. . . .

And they brought young children to him, that he should touch them; and his disciples rebuked those that brought them. But when Jesus saw it, he was much displeased, and said unto them, Suffer the little children to come unto me, and forbid them not; for of such is the kingdom of God. Verily I say unto you, Whosoever shall not receive the kingdom of God as a little child, he shall not enter therein. And he took them up in his arms, put his hands upon them, and blessed them.

—MATTHEW 13; LUKE 10, 15; MARK 10.

Modern Bibles are shown being turned out at the A. J. Holman Bible Co. Inc. of Philadelphia, where the workman is pasting in the end covers of a Bible which, like most other Bibles, was made largely by hand.

THE CHRISTIAN SACRAMENTS

The heart of the faith which began so humbly in the stable at Bethlehem is expressed in the sacraments, for they are based on what Jesus did and said. From infancy to death the sacraments mark the great stages of Christian worship and help the individual worshiper as he experiences some or all of them.

Roman Catholics, the Eastern Orthodox Catholics and many Episcopalians practice all seven sacraments: Baptism, Confirmation, Communion, Marriage, Unction, Penance and Ordination. Some Episcopalians and most Protestants accept only baptism and communion as being divinely instituted by Christ Himself.

A sacrament, said St. Augustine, is the "visible form of an invisible grace." By "grace" St. Augustine meant the overflowing mercy of God, and by "visible form" he meant such facts as receiving water in baptism or bread in communion.

The ways in which the sacraments are observed in various Christian churches are shown on these and the next 16 pages, beginning with baptism.

Even those Protestants who accept some of the sacraments tend to agree with Martin Luther, who said that a "sacrament without testament (words to convey it) is the case without the jewel." A small minority, Quakers and Unitarians among others, accept no sacraments as such, saying that no external act should come between God's will and man.

Russian Orthodox baptism (right) has the officiating priest anointing a baby with oil and then immersing him in the font. The parents do not take part, the baby being held by its godmother. ▶

Baptist service of baptism (left) includes total immersion either in a body of water outdoors or in a tank inside the church. Here the minister lifts a candidate after immersing her. A Baptist must be old enough (usually 12 to 14) to understand the sacrament.

Catholics hold that the sacraments properly given provide grace necessarily and at once. Protestants differ from Catholics by holding that the effects of the sacramental act follow only from the faith of the believer.

But in all the many branches of Christendom, though arguments over the sacraments have split Christendom, the faithful show in their beliefs or their practices the essence of what the sacraments express. "There has never been a week," says a noted Presbyterian minister, "perhaps not a day, since Pentecost that the sacraments have not witnessed to the Christian faith." All Christians everywhere are united in allegiance to what the sacraments represent: the faith kindled 20 centuries ago by the birth of Jesus Christ.

Baptism has always been considered the sacrament of initiation into the Christian church. It is based on the passage near the start of St. Mark's Gospel:

"And it came to pass in those days, that Jesus came from Nazareth of Galilee, and was baptized of John in Jordan. And straightway coming up out of the water, he saw the heavens opened, and the Spirit like a dove descending upon him. And there came a voice from heaven, saying, Thou art my beloved Son, in whom I am well pleased."

Baptism represents the individual's first act of faith, and it seals him as a follower of Christ, washing away previous and original sin (derived from Adam's sin). It is recognized by all churches which accept the sacraments at all.

The greatest thing that ever happens to a Christian is his baptism. According to the social sciences, a human being's main problem in life is to be accepted as an individual person— and not just to be regarded as an "it" among millions of other "its." This struggle is a short one for a Christian; by his baptism he becomes a child of God, called by his own name—his

Congregational baptism: With mother holding baby and father watching, the black-robed minister sprinkles water from a silver bowl on the baby's forehead and says, "I baptize thee in the name of the Father, and of the Son, and of the Holy Ghost."

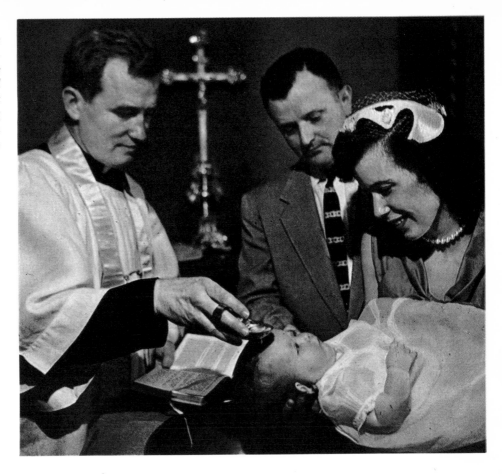

Roman Catholic baptism: After blessing the baby's mouth with salt (for wisdom) and anointing its breast and back with oil (for fortitude), the priest pours water containing holy oil three times on the baby's forehead in the form of a cross.

Christian name. And his Christian name is not simply a way to identify a child; it also emphasizes that he is a person in God's sight and shall remain an individual person for all eternity. His baptismal name sets him off from all other names and for the rest of his life, in the sight of God as well as of other men, he is no longer an "it."

In the words of the Episcopal service of baptism, the person is "baptized with water and the Holy Ghost, and received into Christ's holy Church, and . . . made a living member of the same . . . that he . . . may receive remission of sin, by spiritual regeneration. Receive him, O Lord, as thou hast promised by thy well-beloved Son, saying, Ask, and ye shall have; seek, and ye shall find; knock, and it shall be opened unto you. So give now unto us who ask; . . . that this child may enjoy the everlasting benediction of thy heavenly washing, and may come to the eternal kingdom which thou hast promised by Christ our Lord. . . . and be made an heir of everlasting salvation. . . . Grant that all sinful affections may die in him. . . . We receive this child into the congregation of Christ's flock and do sign him with the sign of the cross, in token that hereafter he shall not be ashamed to confess the faith of Christ crucified, and manfully to fight under his banner, against sin, the world, and the devil; and to continue Christ's faithful soldier and servant unto his life's end. Amen."

Sometimes a few drops are sprinkled on the person being baptized, sometimes water is poured on him, sometimes he is totally immersed. Although most churches baptize at birth, the Baptists and some other groups wait until adolescence or adulthood. All forms of baptism use water and the sign of the cross. And all have the deepest spiritual effect on the baptized. Martin Luther was often shaken in his faith, but in his darkest hours he would repeat the words, *"Baptizatus sum"*—"I have been baptized."

Roman Catholic confirmation (above): *The bishop makes the sign of the cross on the girl's fore-head with chrism (olive oil and balm), saying, ". . . I confirm thee with the chrism of salvation," and blesses her. Then he pats her on the cheek and says, "Peace be with thee." The girl's sponsor stands behind her at the service, which was held in New York City's St. Martin of Tours church.*

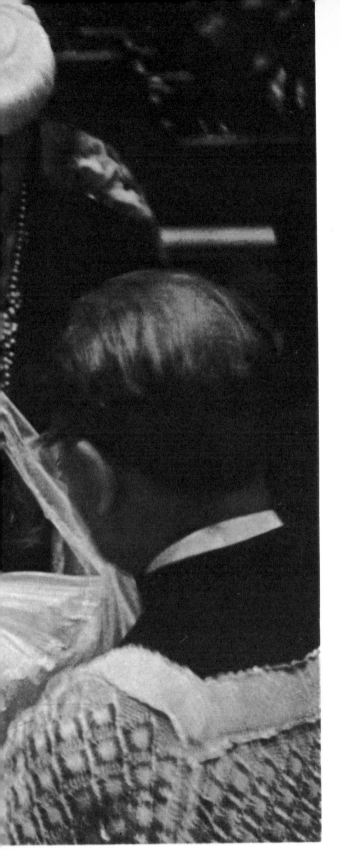

CONFIRMATION: THE SOUL RECEIVES THE HOLY GHOST

Confirmation completes the work of baptism and allows the individual, who is usually between 7 and 14 years old, to assume greater spiritual responsibilities. The sacrament stems from the early evangelistic work of Christ's apostles. "Now when the apostles heard that Samaria had received the word of God, they sent unto them Peter and John: Who . . . prayed for them, that they might receive the Holy Ghost. . . . Then laid they their hands on them, and they received the Holy Ghost" (Acts 8:14–17).

For Roman Catholics and Episcopalians, confirmation is usually performed by a bishop. Because they regard its origin as from the apostles (see Bible passage above) and not divine, Protestants do not recognize confirmation as a sacrament, although Episcopalians call it a "lesser" sacrament. The Lutherans use it not as a sacrament but a rite which reminds children of the covenant made at baptism and also prepares them for first communion.

Lutheran confirmation (right): A girl kneels as the minister says, ". . . for Jesus' sake, renew and increase in thee the gift of the Holy Ghost." He then declares she is a member of the congregation. ▶

COMMUNION FEEDS THE
SOUL OF MAN

The noblest of the sacraments and the one around which all the others revolve is Holy Communion. It re-creates the Last Supper, the climactic meal of Jesus' life, and commemorates His sacrifice for mankind.

At the Last Supper, "as they were eating, Jesus took bread, and blessed it, and brake it, and gave it to the disciples, and said, Take, eat; this is my body. And he took the cup, and gave thanks, and gave it to them, saying, Drink ye all of it; For this is my blood of the new testament, which is shed for many for the remission of sins. But I say unto you, I will not drink henceforth of this fruit of the vine, until that day when I drink it new with you in my Father's kingdom. And when they had sung a hymn, they went out into the mount of Olives" (Matthew 26:26–30).

All the Biblical accounts of the Last Supper make it clear that this meal in the Upper Room in Jerusalem the night before Christ was crucified was to be a source of spiritual strength and help and insight to Christ's followers. Communion has been that ever since.

In taking communion, the worshiper's bread or wafer (which is all that Roman Catholic laymen receive, since the wine is reserved for the priest who conducts the service) represents the body of Christ. Wine, or sometimes grape juice among certain Protestant denominations such as the Methodists, represents Christ's blood. Some groups, especially among the

Presbyterian communion: Members of the congregation remain seated as church elders pass among them with trays containing small glasses of grape juice and cubes of bread which have been consecrated by the minister in a service up at the altar.

Syrian Orthodox communion: By Orthodox custom, children can be confirmed at the time of their baptism and can receive communion immediately afterward from the priest.

Eastern Orthodox churches, take a combination of bread and wine. The Eastern Orthodox have a unique custom, confirming infants and giving them communion directly after baptism.

Roman and Orthodox Catholics, who call the sacrament of communion the Holy Eucharist, believe that when a priest consecrates the bread and wine they are transubstantiated: they become Christ's actual body and blood, their appearance alone remaining as before. Most Protestants believe the body and blood are represented only spiritually, and some Protestants regard communion simply as a memorial act.

One Presbyterian authority writes of the communion service: "The sacrament of the

Roman Catholic communion: Before transubstantiation takes place, the priest raises chalice of wine and water over altar, offering it to God.

Epistle to the Corinthians: "The cup of blessing which we bless, is it not the communion of the blood of Christ? The bread which we break, is it not the communion of the body of Christ?"

St. Paul wrote thus of the Last Supper as part of the message which he was destined to pass on to later Christians; he was a guardian and transmitter of that message. Christian congregations were to observe the communion service until the second coming of Christ. And it was St. Paul, and not the writers of the four Gospels, who introduced the command of Jesus about communion: "This do in remembrance of me."

The whole passage of St. Paul reads: "For I have received of the Lord that which also I delivered unto you, That the Lord Jesus, the same night in which he was betrayed, took bread: And when he had given thanks, he brake it, and said, Take, eat; this is my body, which is broken for you: this do in remembrance of me. After the same manner also he took the cup, when he had supped, saying, This cup is the new testament in my blood; this do ye, as oft as ye drink it, in remembrance of me. For as often as ye eat this bread, and drink this cup, ye do show the Lord's death till he come. Wherefore whosoever shall eat this bread, and drink this cup of the Lord, unworthily, shall be guilty of the body and blood of the Lord. But let a man examine himself, and so let him eat of that bread, and drink of that cup. For he that eateth and drinketh unworthily, eateth and drinketh damnation to himself."

Since Christ sacrificed Himself on the cross to redeem all mankind, and this sacrifice of His body and blood for us is continually recalled in communion, those people who take the communion must always try to be worthy of Jesus. If they take it unworthily they are, as St. Paul

Lord's Supper has one meaning and one message. It commemorates the eternal sacrifice of Christ for us and for our salvation. At the same time, it holds in its keeping all the benefits of the new covenant. It presents to us Christ, and with Christ we receive from His Hands what He has to give."

Different names for this sacrament are found in the New Testament itself. The name "Lord's supper" is derived from Corinthians: "When ye come together therefore into one place, this is not to eat the Lord's supper." The name "communion" also comes from St. Paul's First

says, running into grave danger for themselves.

Communion can be, however, not only the most important and meaningful Christian service but also the most beautiful. Many Christians believe that it lets each individual who takes part in communion have a private and personal meeting with God. Such Christians believe that communion is a joint activity of God and man, a meeting of the whole family of God. The human members of the family thank God for the past, for what He has done, especially in sending His Son to live and die on earth for mankind. They also thank God for the future, both for what they are about to receive in the bread and wine, and for God's lasting benefits to them in this life and the life after death.

So each person who takes part in communion may consider, if he so desires, that he lifts up to God his hopes and fears, his joys and worries, his achievements and failures. And in turn, God can be regarded as bringing down to each person present at communion His life in the sacrament of Christ's body and blood. So each person can offer in communion all that he is and all that he does, fully realizing that he offers imperfect gifts and that he dares to offer them only because of Christ's perfect offering of Himself for humanity.

Yet communion can not only be thought of as a private and personal matter between each single individual and God. It can also be thought of as a supreme act of fellowship among all men—the act of breaking bread together in the Father's house.

Whatever meaning the members of the various Christian churches place on communion, they all agree on its immense significance. For in partaking of Christ's presence a believer partakes of Christ Himself and nourishes his soul for eternal life.

Armenian Apostolic communion (below): *Holding chalice of wine and wafers, the priest places a little on the communicant's tongue.*

MARRIAGE BLESSES
HUMAN LOVE

Marriage is considered a sacrament by Roman Catholics and the Eastern Orthodox Church, some of the latter's services being richly elaborate. Protestants, while not denying marriage's importance, rank it as a ceremony or rite below the sacramental level. To support their belief that Christ authorized Holy Matrimony as a sacrament, Roman Catholics and Orthodox point to His presence at the marriage in Cana of Galilee, where He performed His first miracle. St. Paul added, "Even as Christ also loved the church, and gave himself up for it . . . so ought men to love their wives as their own bodies" (Ephesians: 5:25–28).

In blessing the union of man and woman, marriage sanctifies human love and the procreation and education of children. The churches have always felt some degree of responsibility for education, secular as well as religious. None is more vigilant than the Roman Catholic which operates an entire educational system of its own and specifies that in mixed marriages (i.e., of Catholic and non-Catholic) all children must be brought up within the Roman faith. One Catholic authority describes marriage as "the legitimate and holy union of man and woman for the human race, and the education of children, in the knowledge of religion."

The Roman and Orthodox churches are also more strict than others in their rules concerning divorce, the Roman church forbidding it and permitting permanent separation of man and wife only for extreme causes. Marriage can be voided by annulment, which declares a marriage invalid from the beginning.

Whether it is performed as a sacrament or a simple religious ceremony, marriage is one of the loveliest of all church services. Particularly lovely is the phrasing of the Episcopal Book of Common Prayer which describes matrimony as "an honorable estate, instituted of God." For many the most moving passage of all is the one from the 1662 Anglican prayer book: "With this ring I thee wed; with my body I thee worship, with all my worldly goods I thee endow." These words seal the marriage, the ring at once symbolizing union and eternity.

Methodist marriage (left): *Near end of ceremony the couple kneels at the altar and minister raises his hands over them and pronounces the blessing.*

Greek Orthodox marriage (right): *The best man holds crowns, symbols of equality and virtue, over the heads of the bride and bridegroom.* ▶

Greek Orthodox penance (left): After penitent, kneeling at the front of the church with the priest beside him, has confessed and the priest has asked God for mercy, priest places his stole over penitent's shoulders and pronounces the absolution. Orthodox make confession four or five times a year.

Episcopal penance (below): The minister kneels and leads the congregation in the Litany, beseeching the Lord "to give us true repentance; to forgive us all our sins." The Episcopal General Confession, used more often, includes well-known phrase, ". . . We have left undone those things which we ought to have done; And we have done those things which we ought not to have done. . . . But thou, O Lord, have mercy upon us." Minister then pronounces absolution for all.

SIN IS SHED
BY PENANCE

Mercy and compassion, stemming from the life and character of the Savior Himself, are embodied in the sacrament of penance, in which the Christian confesses his sins and is granted absolution, or formal forgiveness. Penance can be made for specific sins, as by Catholics who confess individually to a single priest (*right*). Or it can be made generally, as by Episcopalians (*below*) in their regular church service even though they do not regard penance as a "greater" sacrament.

Penance springs partly from Christ's powers of healing. He performed miracles not simply to help the suffering but to show His greater mission on earth: to free mankind from the bonds of sin. When he healed a palsied man He said, "Thy sins be forgiven thee" (Matthew 9:2). His death and Resurrection made possible the freeing of the soul from earthly sin. The Christan desire for this is shown in the Lord's Prayer phrase "forgive us our debts."

Roman Catholic penance: A priest leans forward in the confessional to hear clearly the confession being made to him through the screened partition at left. Devout Catholics usually confess once a week. Under no circumstance may a priest use knowledge gained in confession outside the confessional.

Sacraments exist, said John Calvin, to "support the weakness of our faith." This is especially true of penance which presupposes man's continuing sinfulness. Catholics say penance's divine institution comes from Christ's words: "Receive ye the Holy Ghost. Whose sins you shall forgive, they are forgiven them; and whose sins you shall retain, they are retained" (John 20:22–23). Protestants say that although Christ undeniably prescribed penance he did not institute it as a sacrament.

Either as a sacrament or a ceremony, penance has two necessary acts: 1) the confession, which must be accompanied by contrition or sincere repentance, and 2) the absolution. Protestants usually emphasize repentance—some sects making the word "Repent!" almost a battle cry. Catholics place an equal value on absolution, allowing only those who have been absolved to receive communion.

THE SICK FIND SALVATION
THROUGH HOLY UNCTION

"Is any sick among you? let him call for the elders of the church; and let them pray over him, anointing him with oil in the name of the Lord: and the prayer of faith shall save the sick, and the Lord shall raise him up: and if he have committed sins, they shall be forgiven him." So did the Epistle of St. James the Apostle (5:14–15) set forth the theological basis for unction, the sacrament of healing.

Among Roman Catholics, unction is administered only when there is danger of death. Here it is called extreme unction. Completing the work of penance, it assures the soul of grace during its last moments on earth. Although the individual should if possible begin the rite by making confession, this requirement is often passed over if the sick person appears to be near death.

For the Eastern Orthodox Churches, unction can be performed as often as may be necessary to heal and give comfort to the sick in mind and body. It is often administered to the people in their homes (*below*).

Protestants do not regard unction as a sacra-

Rumanian Orthodox unction: In a home a priest, holding a cross, blesses an ailing woman. He anoints each person seven times and each time prays to God, the "physician of souls."

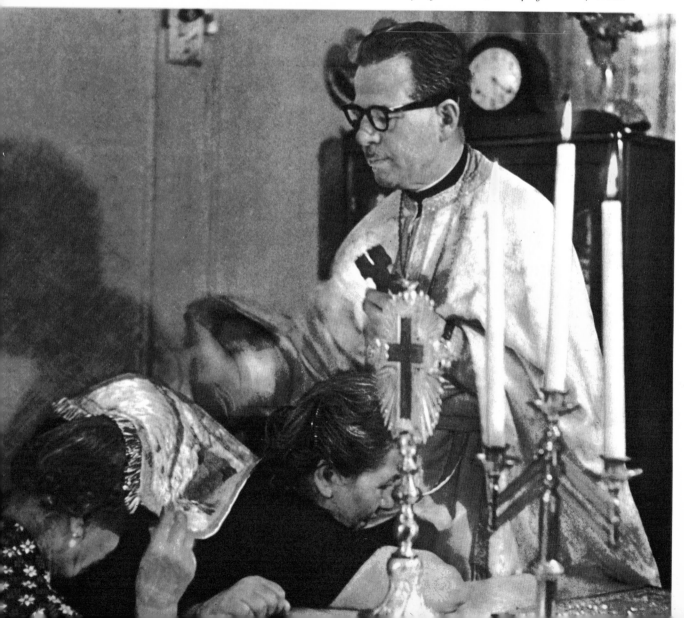

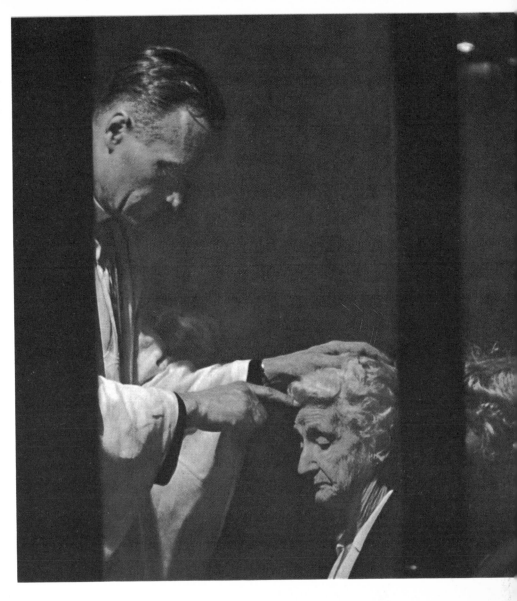

Episcopal unction: A minister lays his hand on the head of an elderly woman at a weekly "Unction of the Sick" service in New York City. He marks a cross on her forehead with holy oil and asks for mercy "that all thy pain and sickness of body being put to flight, the blessing of health may be restored unto thee."

ment. But the Episcopal Church has found increasing acceptance for its unction service, which is given in cooperation with medical authorities. Offered as a "lesser" sacrament, the Episcopal service has helped to reduce physical suffering in a remarkable number of cases, showing once again the spiritual power which for centuries has kept the sacraments at the core of Christian worship.

Roman Catholics believe that unction has four results: remission (that is, forgiveness) of the guilt of sins the person receiving unction may have committed; remission of any remnants of past sin; strengthening of one's soul by arousing confidence in God, thus giving

added power to resist temptation; and the possible return of bodily health.

The Episcopal practice of unction has a long history, but under the impact of modern science the Episcopal service was little used for a great many years. It is a quiet and dignified service which has a regular form in the prayer book. Cures are not promised, and sick persons are advised to seek a physician's help. Its object is to bring all the resources of God's universe to bear upon the sick, not to replace medicine with spiritual healing. Church authorities believe that the close cooperation of religion with doctors and psychiatrists in medical matters is becoming steadily more important.

185

ORDINATION: THE MINISTRY PERPETUATES GOD'S WORD

Just as a sacrament bestows something spiritual, so the power to administer the sacraments is sacred. In the Roman Catholic, Orthodox and Anglican Churches, this power is conferred through the sacrament of ordination, by which higher prelates make ministers or priests.

"As my Father hath sent me," Christ said to His apostles, "even so send I you" (John 20:21). The apostles chose others to ordain and the process has continued in what is called Apostolic Succession for nearly 2,000 years.

In the New Testament, the prophets and teachers of the Church at Antioch marked out Paul and Barnabas for missionary work by laying on their hands. Even Protestants, who state that the Bible does not provide a sacrament of ordination, use the laying on of hands as a meaningful way of handing down the ministry, perpetuating both the church and God's word for all time.

Catholic ordination (below): *Robed in white, candidates prostrate themselves before the altar while a cardinal prays during the service.*

Episcopal ordination (right): *A great cathedral arches above the ordaining of new clergy, one of whom kneels to receive the bishop's blessing.* ▶

CHRISTMAS AND EASTER ARE GREATEST DAYS OF CHRISTIAN YEAR

In Grotto of Nativity in Bethlehem, the traditional site of Christ's birth is marked by a silver star with a hole that permits pilgrims who so desire to kiss the original rock floor. ▶

In Bethlehem, Christian priests and ministers speak many languages. For this is a place that is holy to Christians of all lands and groups— Orthodox, Catholic and Protestant. Through the ages, pilgrims have come to Bethlehem in reverence and love, for here Christ was born in a stable on the first Christmas day.

In Jerusalem, not far from Bethlehem in the Holy Land, Christ ended his earthly life on the cross on Good Friday, and three days later rose triumphant from the tomb on the first Easter. The star of Bethlehem and the cross of Calvary are still the symbols of Christian faith and still celebrate the greatest events of Christianity: the Savior's birth, agony and Resurrection.

No other days mean as much to Christians, though festivals do mark many times like the Ascension and the coming of the wise men.

Christmas and Easter, the two greatest days of the Christian year, are celebrated in many ways in different countries. The Christmas tree, topped by its star, rich with decorations and surrounded by gifts for all members of the family especially the children, was popular in Germany long before it became popular in the United States. The Easter bunny and the Easter egg take various forms; the most elaborate eggs of all are probably those of Eastern Europe, including Russia. The church services that mark these two great days can range from a colorful midnight Mass at Christmas with thousands of people crowded into a great cathedral to a quiet Easter sunrise service in an open field. But binding all worshipers together—as it binds the whole Christian world together— is the one faith kindled in the Holy Land 20 centuries ago by the life, the redeeming death and the Resurrection of Jesus Christ.

INDEX

PICTURE SOURCES

Pictures on each page are listed from left to right and from top to bottom. Photographic listings are followed by the name of the photographer or agency.

1, 5, 6 Michelangelo Frescoes. Frank Lerner, Courtesy The Vatican

INTRODUCTION

8 Animist-Hindu Cremation, Bali. Ewing Krainin
9 Honoring a Guru. Marc Riboud
10 Jain Sacred Statue. James Burke
11 Pilgrims at Shinto Shrine, Kyoto. Ewing Krainin
  Sikhs at Golden Temple, Amritsar. Marc Riboud
12 Syncretist Lecture. Leonard McCombe

HINDUISM

13-34 The Spirit of Hinduism. Photographs by Leonard McCombe, with the exception of
20-21 Hindu Gods and Demons. Illust. by Boris Artzybasheff

BUDDHISM

35-56 The Path of Buddhism. Photographs by Howard Sochurek, except as noted
40 Pilgrims at Bo Tree. T. S. Satyan
41 Reclining Buddha Statue. Eliot Elisofon
42 Wheel of the Law. Illustration by Antonio Petruccelli
48-49 Spread of Buddhism. Map by Antonio Petruccelli
50 Kuan Yin, Goddess of Mercy. Courtesy Boston Museum of Fine Arts
51 Amitabha Buddha. K. Tateishi
55 Japanese Priest. Jun Miki
56 Tibetan War Dance. James Burke

CONFUCIANISM—TAOISM

57 Taoist Priest. Howard Sochurek

58 Guardian Image. Dmitri Kessel
60 Memorial Birthday Rites. Howard Sochurek
61 Yang and Yin. Illustration by Antonio Petruccelli
62 Boat for the Gods. Howard Sochurek
63 Dragon Procession. Howard Staples
64 Revering Ancestors. Howard Sochurek
65 Revering Ancestors. Ewing Krainin
66 Lao Tzu. Howard Sochurek, Courtesy Joint Administration of National Museums and Library, Formosa
67 Descendant of Confucius. Howard Sochurek
68 Confucius as Teacher. Howard Sochurek, Courtesy Joint Admin. of National Museums and Library, Formosa
69 Temple of Confucius. Ergy Landau from Rapho-Guillumette
70-71 Birthday of Confucius. Horace Bristol
72 Confucian Virtues. Howard Sochurek, Courtesy Joint Administration of National Museums and Library, Formosa
74-75 Reception of Immortals. Larry Burrows, Courtesy British Museum
76 Burning of Paper House. Howard Sochurek

ISLAM

77-96 The World of Islam. Photographs by David Douglas Duncan, except as noted
78 Shiite Mosque. Dmitri Kessel
80 Mount of Mercy. Abdul Ghafur Sheikh
86 Plain of Arafat. Djemal Tchanderli
87 The Great Mosque of Mecca. M. Afzal Malik

88-89 Moslem World. Map by Antonio Petruccelli
93 Sufi Leader. Herbert Orth, Courtesy Metropolitan Museum of Art
96 Miniature Tomb of Husein. James Burke

JUDAISM

97 Reading the Torah. Alfred Eisenstaedt
98-117 The Law of Judaism. Photographs by Cornell Capa from Magnum, except as noted
101 Discovery Site of Dead Sea Scrolls. James Whitmore.
102 Repairing the Torah. Alfred Eisenstaedt
103 Blowing Ram's Horn. Alfred Eisenstaedt
104-105 Jewish Family Life. Alfred Eisenstaedt
106 Sabbath Blessing. Alfred Eisenstaedt
107 Confirmation. Alfred Eisenstaedt
108-109 Jewish Family Life. Burton Glinn from Magnum
111-113 Passover. Alfred Eisenstaedt, except page 112, lower left
114-115 Elders in Israel Synagogue. Alfred Eisenstaedt
118 Israel. Alfred Eisenstaedt

CHRISTIANITY

119 Werden Crucifix. Dmitri Kessel
120 National Cathedral Choir. Gjon Mili
121 Apostles' Creed. Illuminated manuscript by Daisy Alcock
122-123 Adoration of the Holy Child. Dmitri Kessel, Courtesy Uffizi Galleries, Florence
124 Temptation in the Wilderness, Baptism in the Jordan. Dmitri Kessel, Courtesy Scuola di San Rocco, Venice, and National Gallery, London

TEXT SOURCES

Special acknowledgment is also made to the following publishers for their permission to quote copyrighted material used in this book, especially in the selections of writings of the various faiths. In some instances, different translations have been combined or the wordings slightly changed for accuracy or clarity. Spellings in the book conform with common Western usage.

ABHEDANANDA, SWAMI (comp.)—*The Sayings of Sri Ramakrishna.* N. Y.: Vedanta Society, 1903.

BREWSTER, EARL H. (ed.)—*The Life of Gotama the Buddha.* London: Routledge & Kegan Paul, 1926.

BROWNE, LEWIS (transl.)—*The Wisdom of Israel.* Random House, 1945.

BURNELL, A. C. (transl.)—*The Ordinances of Manu.* London: Routledge & Kegan Paul, 1891.

BURTT, E. A. (ed.)—*The Teachings of The Compassionate Buddha.* New American Library, 1955.

CAMPBELL, W. L. (transl.)—*The Tree of Wisdom.* Calcutta: Calcutta Univ. at the Baptist Mission Press, 1919.

CARUS, PAUL (transl.)—*The Gospel of Buddha.* La Salle, Ill.: Open Court Pub. Co., 1917.

CATHOLIC STUDENTS' MISSION CRUSADE, U.S.A. —"Catholic Students' Mission Crusade World Mission Map." Cincinnati: Catholic Students' Mission Crusade, U.S.A., National Center, 1956.

CONZE, EDWARD (ed.)—*Buddhist Texts through the Ages.* Oxford: Cassirer, 1954.

DAVIDS, C. A. F. RHYS (transl. and ed.)—*Psalms of the Early Buddhists.* London: Pali Text Society, 1909.

DAVIDS, T. W. RHYS (transl.) and C. A. F. RHYS (ed.)—*Buddhist Birth Stories* (Jataka tales). London: Routledge and Kegan Paul, 1925.

DAVIDS, T. W. RHYS and C. A. F. RHYS (ed.)— *The Sacred Books of the Buddhists.* London: Pali Text Society, 1910, 1921.

DUTT, MANMATHA NATH (ed.)—*The Garuda Purana.* Calcutta: Soc. for the Resuscitation of Indian Lit., 1908.

EVANS-WENTZ, W. Y. (ed.)—*Tibetan Yoga and Secret Doctrines.* London: Oxford U. P., 1935.

GODDARD, DWIGHT (ed.)—*A Buddhist Bible.* Dutton, 1938.

GRIFFITH, RALPH T. H. (transl.)—*Hymns of the Atharva-Veda.* Benares: Lazarus, 1895.

GRIFFITH, RALPH T. H. (transl.)—*Hymns of the Rig-Veda.* Benares: Lazarus, 1896.

GRUBB, KENNETH G. (ed.) and E. J. BINGLE (assoc. ed.)—*World Christian Handbook, 1952 Edition.* London: World Dominion Press, 1952.

HAMILTON, CLARENCE H. (ed.)—*Buddhism. A Religion of Infinite Compassion.* N. Y.: Liberal Arts Press, 1952.

HERTZ, RABBI JOSEPH H.—*The Authorized Daily Prayer Book.* N.Y.: Bloch Pub. Co., 1955.

JEWISH PUBLICATION SOCIETY OF AMERICA— *The Holy Scriptures According to the Masoretic Text.* Philadelphia: 1955.

LANDIS, BENSON Y. (ed.)—*Yearbook of American Churches for 1957.* N. Y.: Nat. Council of the Churches of Christ in the U.S.A., 1956.

LIN YUTANG (transl. and ed.)—*The Wisdom of Laotse.* Random House, 1948.

MADHAVANANDA, SWAMI (transl.)—*The Brihadaranyaka Upanishad.* Almora: Advaita Ashrama, 3rd ed., 1950.

MORGAN, KENNETH W. (ed.)—*The Religion of the Hindus.* Translations from Sanskrit by V. Raghavan. N. Y.: Ronald, 1953.

MULLER, F. MAX (transl.)—*Lectures on the Science of Religion.* Scribner's, 1872.

MULLER, F. MAX (ed.)—*The Sacred Books of the East.* Oxford: Clarendon, 1879-1910.

NEWMAN, RABBI LOUIS I. (transl.), with the collaboration of Samuel Spitz—*Talmudic Anthology.* N. Y.: Behrman House, 1945.

NIKHILANANDA, SWAMI (transl.)—*The Upanishads.* Vol. I. Harper, 1949.

PICKTHALL, MOHAMMED MARMADUKE (transl.) —*The Meaning of the Glorious Koran.* London: Allen & Unwin, 1930.

PRABHAVANANDA, SWAMI, AND ISHERWOOD, CHRISTOPHER (transl.) — *Bhagavad-Gita: The Song of God.* Hollywood: Marcel Rodd, 1944.

REICHELT, KARL LUDVIG—*Truth and Tradition in Chinese Buddhism.* (transl.) Kathrina van Wagenen Bugge. Shanghai: Commercial Press, 1927.

STEINBERG, MILTON—*Basic Judaism.* Harcourt, Brace, 1947.

THOMAS, E. J. (transl.)—*Buddhist Scriptures.* London: John Murray, 1913.

WALEY, ARTHUR (transl.) — *The Analects of Confucius.* London: Allen & Unwin, 2nd ed., 1945.

WARREN, HENRY CLARKE (transl.)—*Buddhism in Translations, Vol. 3, Harvard Oriental Series.* Cambridge: Harvard U. P., 1947.

WOODWARD, F. L. (transl.)—*Minor Anthologies of the Pali Canon. Part II.* London: Oxford U. P., 1935.